IT'S NOT ROCKET SCIENCE

In the same series

How to Boil an Egg . . . and 184 other simple recipes for one
No Meat for Me, Please!

Uniform with this book

Where to find *Right Way*

Elliot *Right Way* take pride in our editorial quality, accuracy and value-for-money. Booksellers everywhere can rapidly obtain any *Right Way* book for you. If you have been particularly pleased with any one title, do please mention this to your bookseller as personal recommendation helps us enormously.

Please send to the address on the back of the title page opposite, a stamped, self-addressed envelope if you would like a copy of our *free catalogue*. Alternatively, you may wish to browse through our extensive range of informative titles arranged by subject on the Internet at **www.right-way.co.uk**

We welcome views and suggestions from readers as well as from prospective authors; do please write to us or e-mail: **info@right-way.co.uk**

IT'S NOT ROCKET SALAD!

AFFORDABLE MEAT-FREE RECIPES FOR STUDENTS

Viv Swallow

RIGHT WAY

Copyright notice

© Elliot Right Way Books MMVI

All rights reserved. No part of this book may be reproduced, stored in a retrieval system, or transmitted, in any form or by any means, electronic, photocopying, mechanical, recording or otherwise, without the prior permission of the copyright owner.

Conditions of sale
This book shall only be sold, lent, or hired, for profit, trade, or otherwise, in its original binding, except where special permission has been granted by the Publisher.

Whilst care is taken in selecting Authors who are authoritative in their subjects, it is emphasised that their books can reflect their knowledge only up to the time of writing. Information can be superseded and printers' errors can creep in. This book is sold, therefore, on the condition that neither Publisher nor Author can be held legally responsible for the consequences of any error or omission there may be.

Typeset in 10/11 pt Swiss 721 by Letterpart Ltd., Reigate, Surrey.

Printed and bound in Great Britain by Cox & Wyman Ltd., Reading, Berkshire.

The *Right Way* series is published by Elliot Right Way Books, Brighton Road, Lower Kingswood, Tadworth, Surrey, KT20 6TD, U.K. For information about our company and the other books we publish, visit our website at www.right-way.co.uk

CONTENTS

CHAPTER	PAGE
Introduction	7
1. Starters, Snacks & Light Meals	11
2. Potato Dishes	37
3. Pasta Dishes	55
4. Main Courses	71
Index	125

INTRODUCTION

This recipe collection was not assembled with publication in mind! It began when my daughter, at the tender age of eight, announced that she didn't want to eat meat any more. Fine, I thought, I can go along with this and waited for the inevitable request for a bacon sandwich. When it didn't come, I realised that I would have to give more consideration to family meals.

So, over the years, I tried many variations of vegetarian and meat-free recipes, adapting and changing favourite recipes to omit the meat and introduce different combinations of flavours. By the time my daughter had reached the age of eighteen, the collection had been tried and tweaked, and had grown to the size it is now.

Before she went to university we shopped for a simple meat-free cookery book as it dawned on us that, in shared student accommodation, she was likely to be surrounded by carnivores and would have to cater for herself.

Although there are many vegetarian and meat-free books on the market, we couldn't find just what we were looking for. The recipes needed to:

a) contain nutritious ingredients
b) be relatively cheap and easy to cook
c) use ingredients that are tasty and widely available
d) range from simple to impressive
e) be adaptable regarding quantities
f) be appealing!

The simple solution was to present my recipes to her in a folder, so that is what I did. Now, towards the end of her first year at university, she has successfully prepared the recipes herself and has even converted some of her meat-eating friends.

As all mothers know, it is a fairly straightforward task to ensure your children have a balanced diet at home. When they leave the nest, however, it can be a different story: there are a thousand things to consider and it is possible that dietary considerations might not be top of the list. I don't pretend that all the recipes in this book are fat-free/high in fibre/low in cholesterol, etc., but when eaten as part of a balanced diet with plenty of fresh fruit and vegetables a healthy level can be achieved.

These days there is far greater emphasis on planning a healthy diet. The initiative of 'Five A Day' (making sure you consume at least five portions of fresh fruit and vegetables each day) underlines the benefits of eating unprocessed foods. Fruit and vegetables are packed with nutrients and vitamins, and research has shown that a balanced meat-free diet can also lower the risk of heart disease and cancer.

Of course, it is also possible to go wrong when excluding meat from your diet. For all of us to be healthy we need to consume the correct balance of protein, fats, carbohydrates, minerals and vitamins, or we can find ourselves in trouble. When following a meat-free regime it is important to understand the following. Fatigue is something that can hit, and may indicate that you are not eating enough protein. Foods such as yoghurt, milk, eggs, nuts (if you are not allergic), etc., are high in protein, so make sure they form a regular part of your diet.

Iron deficiency can also cause tiredness and anaemia, and sceptics often believe that vegetarians are more prone to this than meat-eaters. Good sources of iron are wholemeal products, spinach, dried apricots, pulses and beans.

There is temptation too, when avoiding meat, to compensate by upping the amount of carbohydrate you consume. Products like pasta, white rice and pastries are usually high in carbohydrate and, whilst we need this for energy, too much can lead to weight gain and digestive problems. Try substituting white rice with wild or brown rice occasionally and white pasta with wholemeal as these contain more fibre. This aids digestion and may help to reduce the risk of heart disease and diabetes. Healthfood shops also sell vitamin supplements designed specifically for vegetarians, but anyone whether vegetarian or otherwise should consult his or her doctor if experiencing unexplained tiredness or other symptoms of ill health.

The social life of students is very important, and it is

unlikely that they will want to spend hours in the kitchen preparing meals. In recognition of this, the first section of the book is devoted to Starters, Snacks and Light Meals. There will be times when something quick and tasty is required and the recipes here are designed for that purpose. There is also a section for Potatoes, with recipes ranging from jacket potatoes with various fillings to more substantial dishes to be eaten with other accompaniments. Ever popular Pasta deserved a section in its own right with quick pour-over sauces and dishes to be oven-baked. The largest section relates to Main Meals with a wide variety of dishes to try. In this section (as with the others), it is possible to cook for smaller or larger numbers by amending the ingredient amounts accordingly. It would be quite simple to prepare an impressive dinner party by serving fellow students with, for example, a simple starter followed by a dish of pasta with sauce and garlic bread, or Nutty Stilton Tart with Rocket Salad. Alternatively, invite your mates around for Sweet and Savoury Kebabs with tortilla chips and dips. There are many different combinations to try.

The recipes in this book are *meat-free* not vegetarian. The reason for this is that some of the recipes incorporate tuna and some use cheeses that are not vegetarian. Non-vegetarian cheeses are made using rennet, which is an animal extract. Vegetarian cheese is made by using artificially produced rennet. In most of the recipes it would be possible to substitute the cheeses stated for vegetarian varieties when they are available.

So, for the days when inspiration just won't come and baked beans or a plain salad just doesn't appeal, try one of the recipes in this book – after all, 'It's not Rocket Science'!

STARTERS, SNACKS & LIGHT MEALS

Mozzarella Melts

Serves 4

**4 small ciabatta rolls
100g pesto
250g cherry tomatoes, halved
75g pitted black and green olives, sliced
350g mozzarella cheese, sliced
extra virgin olive oil**

To serve:
fresh torn basil leaves

Cut each roll in half and spread each half with the pesto. Add the tomato halves, olives and cheese, then drizzle with olive oil.

Grill under a high heat for about 7 minutes, until the cheese is golden.

Serve dressed with some torn basil leaves.

Tomato Brunch

Makes 4 slices

**6 tomatoes, thickly sliced
olive oil
4 thick slices of soda bread
balsamic vinegar
salt and black pepper
small amount of grated cheese**

Gently fry the tomato slices in some olive oil in a frying pan until softened and beginning to brown.

Lightly toast the soda bread under a hot grill, then place the tomatoes on each slice. Drizzle each slice lightly with olive oil and balsamic vinegar, season to taste then lightly scatter with the cheese.

Grill a little longer until the cheese begins to melt. Serve immediately.

Banana Grills

Makes 4 slices

**4 thick slices of wholemeal bread
115g soft crème fraîche
3 bananas, sliced
4 tsp honey or golden syrup**

---   ---

Toast the bread under the grill on one side only. Spread the untoasted side with the crème fraîche.

Arrange the banana slices on top, then drizzle each slice with the honey/golden syrup.

Pop back under the hot grill until hot and bubbling.

---   ---

Mushrooms in Garlic Butter

Serves 2

**100g butter
1 large garlic clove, peeled and crushed
18 button mushrooms**

To serve:
4 chunks of crusty bread

Warm two small shallow dishes in the oven at 100°C (gas mark ½).

Melt the butter in a frying pan and add the crushed garlic, then fry the mushrooms until cooked.

Divide the mushrooms and butter between the warmed dishes and serve with the crusty bread to mop up the garlic butter.

Cheese and Apple Snacks

Serves 2

**2 Cox's apples
lemon juice
200g cheese, grated
Worcestershire sauce
4 slices of bread
50g butter or margarine
25g chopped nuts (optional)**

Core one of the apples and cut into eight thin rings, then cover with some lemon juice to prevent browning. Peel and grate the remaining apple then mix with the cheese and a few drops of Worcestershire sauce.

Toast the bread then butter it, and cover each slice with the cheese mixture. Sprinkle with the chopped nuts and garnish each slice with two apple rings.

Put back under a hot grill until the cheese starts to bubble.

Mozzarella and Cranberry Toasts

Serves 1

**2 thick slices of rustic bread
2 tsp cranberry sauce
100g ball of mozzarella cheese
olive oil
salt and pepper**

To serve:
**rocket leaves
balsamic vinegar**

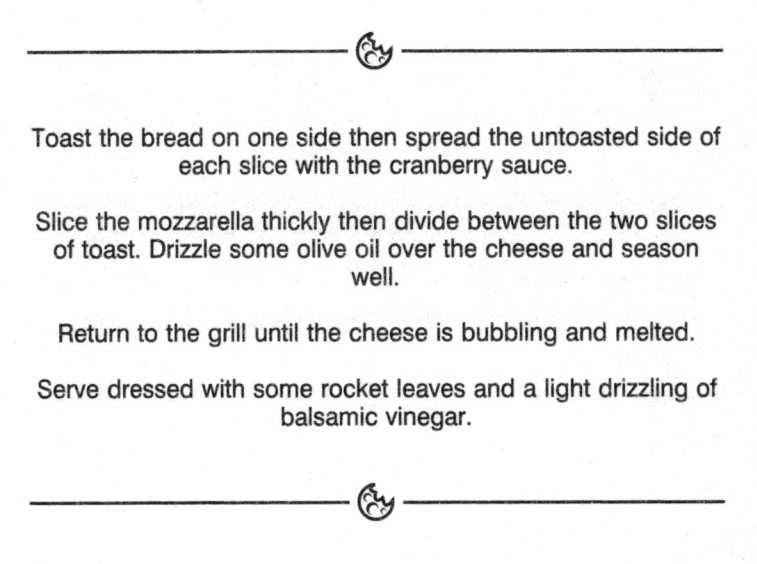

Toast the bread on one side then spread the untoasted side of each slice with the cranberry sauce.

Slice the mozzarella thickly then divide between the two slices of toast. Drizzle some olive oil over the cheese and season well.

Return to the grill until the cheese is bubbling and melted.

Serve dressed with some rocket leaves and a light drizzling of balsamic vinegar.

Pineapple Toasties

Serves 2

**4 slices of wholemeal bread
5 pineapple rings
100g Lancashire cheese, grated
1 green pepper, de-seeded and finely chopped
125g natural yoghurt
salt and pepper**

Lightly toast the bread.

Chop one of the pineapple rings then mix together with the cheese, green pepper and yoghurt, then season.

Spread the mixture over the toast slices and top each with a pineapple ring.

Place under a hot grill until the pineapple is warmed through and the cheese is beginning to brown.

Pepper Pesto Toasties

Serves 2

**6 slices of bloomer bread
1 yellow pepper, de-seeded and sliced
1 red onion, peeled and thinly sliced
olive oil for grilling
6 tblsp mayonnaise
2 tblsp pesto
salt and black pepper**

Preheat the grill and toast the bread lightly on both sides.

Then lay the pepper and onion slices in a grill pan, drizzle with olive oil and grill for 5 minutes.

Mix the mayonnaise with the pesto and spread on the toasted slices. Arrange the pepper and onion slices so they overlap each other on the toast.

Season well, drizzle with a little more olive oil, then heat through under the hot grill.

Tomato and Mushroom Bruschetta

Serves 2

**5 tblsp olive oil
4 large tomatoes, sliced
4 slices of thick wholemeal bread, toasted
8 button mushrooms, sliced
1 garlic clove, peeled and crushed**

To garnish:
black pepper and fresh basil leaves (optional)

Heat the oil in a frying pan, add the sliced tomatoes and fry for 4–5 minutes until softened.

Divide the tomatoes between the wholemeal toast and keep warm under a low grill.

Add the mushrooms and garlic to the pan and fry until cooked and golden. Spoon the mushrooms and oil over the tomatoes.

Season with black pepper and garnish with some basil leaves.

Eggy Bread

Serves 1-2

**2 eggs
75ml milk
salt and pepper
margarine for frying
3–4 slices of white bread**

To serve:
Worcestershire sauce

Beat the eggs and milk together in a bowl and season well, then melt some margarine over a low heat in a frying pan.

Tip the egg mixture into a large dish and lay the bread slices into the mixture, coating thoroughly. (Don't leave the slices in for too long though, or they will 'drink' all the mixture!)

Next fry the bread, one slice at a time until golden brown. Serve with Worcestershire sauce.

Bruschetta with Olives and Cherry Tomatoes

Serves 2–3

**9–10 slices of ciabatta bread
olive oil
1 garlic clove, peeled
half a jar of pitted black olives
1 small pack of cherry tomatoes
salt and pepper**

To serve:
rocket leaves

Toast the ciabatta slices lightly under a hot grill, then drizzle lightly with olive oil and rub with the garlic. Crush the olives and cherry tomatoes together and spread over the bread slices and season.

Drizzle with more olive oil, place on a baking tray and cook in the oven at 160°C (gas mark 3) for about 10 minutes.

To serve, season, top with some rocket leaves and a little more olive oil.

Mushroom Grill

Serves 1

**4 flat mushrooms
olive oil
1 tsp Marmite dissolved in 1 tblsp of water
100g cottage cheese
2 tblsp Edam cheese, grated
½ tsp English mustard
2 slices of granary bread
butter**

Remove the stalks and place the mushrooms on a grill pan, drizzle with a little olive oil and cook for 5 minutes.

Remove from the grill then pour the Marmite mixture over the top.

Mix together the cheeses and mustard and place some of the mixture in each mushroom, then grill for 5–6 minutes until warmed through.

Meanwhile, toast the bread and butter it whilst still warm. Serve the mushrooms on the warm toast.

Hot Halloumi with Tomatoes

Serves 4

**2 large beef tomatoes
2 tblsp fresh mint, chopped
olive oil
salt and pepper
100g halloumi cheese
flour**

***To serve:*
ciabatta bread**

Slice the tomatoes and arrange on individual serving plates, sprinkle with the mint, drizzle with oil and season.

Cut the halloumi into thick slices and flour on both sides.

Heat some oil in a frying pan and fry the cheese slices until golden.

Drain on kitchen paper, then serve on top of the tomato slices.

This dish makes a nice light lunch when served with ciabatta bread.

Tomato Salsa and Tzatziki with Tortilla Chips

Serves 4

**½ cucumber, diced
200g set natural yoghurt
1 tblsp mint sauce
3 tomatoes, finely chopped
4 sun-dried tomatoes, finely chopped
1 onion, peeled and finely chopped
2 tsp of sun-dried tomato olive oil**

To serve:
tortilla chips

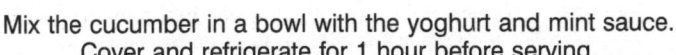

Mix the cucumber in a bowl with the yoghurt and mint sauce. Cover and refrigerate for 1 hour before serving.

Mix the tomatoes (fresh and sun-dried), onion and oil in a bowl, cover and refrigerate as above.

Serve with large bowls of different flavoured tortilla chips – *party food*!

Grilled Ricotta with Sun-Dried Tomatoes

Serves 2–3

1 baguette
250g ricotta cheese
olive oil
10g flat leaf parsley, chopped
1 tsp pesto
1 tblsp lemon juice
50g sun-dried tomatoes in olive oil, chopped
½ garlic clove, peeled and crushed

Cut the baguette into thick diagonal slices. Thickly spread the ricotta on each bread slice. Drizzle with a little olive oil and grill until the cheese begins to brown and melt.

Meanwhile, place the remaining ingredients in a bowl and mix well together. Add some sun-dried tomato olive oil and mix to a salad-dressing consistency.

Remove the bread slices from the grill and place on individual plates. Spoon the dressing over and serve immediately.

Mushroom Brunch

Serves 2

½ onion, peeled and finely chopped
250g button mushrooms
1 garlic clove, peeled and crushed
olive oil for frying
1 tblsp lemon juice
salt and pepper
1 tblsp fresh parsley, chopped
4 potato farls
2 large eggs

To garnish:
1 tblsp chopped chives

Fry the onion, mushrooms and garlic together in a little olive oil in a frying pan, then add the lemon juice and season to taste. Add the parsley, keeping on a low heat.

Toast the potato farls and keep them warm.

Carefully break the eggs into a saucepan half filled with boiling water and poach for 3 minutes until cooked. Put two farls on each plate, then top with the mushroom mixture and a poached egg.

Garnish with the chives and serve immediately.

Panini Parcels

Serves 2

**2 small panini
1 tblsp pesto
1 red pepper, de-seeded and finely sliced
1 large tomato, finely chopped
1 stick of celery, finely chopped
1 tblsp sweetcorn
4 sun-dried tomatoes, chopped
50g crumbly blue cheese
50g mozzarella cheese, sliced
olive oil**

Preheat the oven to 200°C (gas mark 6).

Halve the panini, place the bottoms, cut-side-up, on two squares of foil and spread with the pesto.

Next layer the pepper, tomato, celery, sweetcorn, sun-dried tomatoes and blue cheese on top, and finish with the sliced mozzarella.

Drizzle well with olive oil, then replace the tops of the panini and wrap them in foil. Place on a baking tray and cook in the oven for approximately 15 minutes until hot and the cheese has melted.

Celery and Onion Ramekins

Makes 3

2 sticks of celery, chopped
1 onion, peeled and finely chopped
oil to cook
2 level tblsp plain flour
50g butter
250ml milk
salt and pepper
75g cheese, grated
1 slice of freshly grated breadcrumbs

Cook the celery and onion in some oil in a frying pan until softened but not brown.

In a small saucepan heat the flour, butter and milk together, stirring constantly to prevent sticking. Once the mixture is smooth, season to taste, then add the celery and onion to the sauce mix and stir well together.

Divide the mixture between greased ramekin dishes, then mix the grated cheese and breadcrumbs together and spread over the top.

Bake in the oven at 180°C (gas mark 4), until bubbling and the breadcrumb mixture is browned (approximately 12–15 minutes).

Mushroom Hollows

Serves 2

**1 small French stick cut in half, then in half lengthways
olive oil for cooking
250g small button mushrooms, cut in half
1 garlic clove, peeled and crushed
3 tblsp vegetable stock
3 tblsp lemon juice
2 tblsp milk
3 tblsp chopped chives
salt and pepper**

Scoop out the centre of the bread pieces, leaving a border around the edge of the crust. Brush the bread shells with olive oil, place on a baking tray then bake in the oven at 200°C (gas mark 6) for about 6 minutes, until crisp and golden.

In a small saucepan, bring to the boil the mushrooms with the garlic, stock, lemon juice and milk, then simmer for 5 minutes. Remove the mushroom mixture from the heat and add the chives and seasoning.

Spoon the mushroom mixture into the bread hollows, pouring the remaining mixture on the top. Serve hot.

Red Onion Soup with Cheese Rafts

Serves 4

**3 red onions, peeled and sliced
oil for cooking
1 tsp chopped fresh coriander (optional)
1 tblsp flour, mixed with a little cold water to form a smooth paste
1 litre vegetable stock
1 tblsp tomato purée
½ glass red wine
salt and pepper
2 slices of white bread
grated cheese**

Fry the onions in some oil in a large saucepan until soft and dark, stirring constantly to prevent sticking.

Remove from the heat and stir in the coriander and flour mixture. Then add the vegetable stock, tomato purée, wine and seasoning and simmer until the soup has thickened.

Lightly toast the bread then spread with some grated cheese and grill until the cheese melts. Cut into triangles.

To serve, ladle the soup into individual dishes and float the cheese rafts on the top.

Hot Avocado with Brie

Serves 4 as a starter

**2 large avocados, halved and stoned
1 tblsp lemon juice
175g Brie, thinly sliced**

Brush the cut side of the avocado with the lemon juice to prevent discoloration.

Put the sliced Brie in the hollows.

Cook under a hot grill until the cheese is bubbling and the avocado is warmed through. Serve straight away.

Courgette and Cream Cheese Pâté

**100g courgette, finely chopped
1 red onion, peeled and finely chopped
1 garlic clove, peeled and finely chopped
2 tblsp olive oil
180g full-fat soft cheese
50g toasted almonds, very finely chopped (optional)**

Fry the courgette, onion and garlic together in the olive oil in a frying pan until brown and softened. Leave to cool, then mix well with the cream cheese and almonds. Transfer to a serving dish and chill in the refrigerator.

Mushroom Pâté

1 small onion, peeled and finely chopped
140g butter
225g mushrooms, finely chopped
25g fresh breadcrumbs
100g full-fat soft cheese
1 tsp lemon juice
salt and black pepper

Sauté the onion in the butter in a frying pan for 5 minutes. Add the mushrooms and sauté for a further 5 minutes. Remove from the heat and add the remaining ingredients and mix well. The mixture can be left coarse, or blended in a food processor for a smoother pâté. Spoon into a serving dish. Chill in the refrigerator before serving.

Tuna Pâté

1 small can of tuna, drained
100g full-fat soft cheese
knob of butter
1 tsp lemon juice
salt and black pepper

To garnish:
cucumber slices

Mix together well in a bowl all the ingredients except the cucumber. Spoon into a serving dish and chill in the refrigerator before serving. Garnish with the cucumber.

Cheese, Celery and Onion Pancakes

Serves 4

125g plain flour
1 egg
300ml milk
225g cheese, grated
3 sprigs fresh parsley, finely chopped
butter for cooking
175g celery, chopped
350g onion, peeled and chopped
2 tsp wholegrain mustard
4 tblsp double cream
salt and pepper

Put the flour in a bowl and beat in the egg, then add the milk a little at a time until the mixture is smooth. Next, add 50g cheese and the parsley to the batter mix. Heat a little butter in a non-stick frying pan, pour in a little batter, tipping the pan until there is a thin coating of the batter across the base. Cook until the pancake begins to lift at the edges, then ease gently over to cook the other side. Continue making the pancakes, transferring them to a warm plate, until all the batter is used.

Sauté the celery and onion in butter until soft then remove from the heat. Stir in the mustard, cream, 125g cheese, then season to taste. Divide the mixture and spread over the pancakes. Roll up each pancake and place side by side in a shallow ovenproof dish. Sprinkle the remaining cheese over the top, then place in the oven at 190°C (gas mark 5) for 10–15 minutes.

Tomato and Mushroom Pancakes

Use the same ingredients as opposite except substitute the celery, onion and mustard with 4 large chopped tomatoes and 100g chopped mushrooms.

Make up the pancakes as opposite, then fry the chopped tomatoes with the chopped mushrooms, season well and stir in 4 tblsp double cream. Fill the pancakes, roll up, sprinkle with the cheese and cook as opposite.

Salsa Nachos

Serves 2–3

**200g bag of tortilla chips – either plain or flavoured
300g jar of salsa
4 spring onions, trimmed and finely chopped
½ red pepper, de-seeded and very finely chopped
175g cheese, grated**

Spread the tortilla chips over a large grill pan or baking tray, then spread the salsa over the top.

Sprinkle the spring onions and red pepper over, then top with the grated cheese.

Heat under a hot grill until the cheese starts to bubble – do not overcook. Serve immediately.

Home-Made Onion Rings with Pink Coleslaw

Serves 4

For the onion rings:
100g plain flour
salt and pepper
2 eggs, beaten
oil for deep frying
150ml milk
2 Spanish onions

For the coleslaw:
250g red cabbage, finely sliced
250g white cabbage, finely sliced
25g onion (white or red), peeled and finely sliced
10ml lemon juice
black pepper
120g mayonnaise

Take extra care when deep-fat frying. Hot oil spits wildly and can rise up the sides of the pan very quickly.

Put the flour in a large bowl and season. Make a well in the centre of the flour and add the beaten eggs and 1 tblsp of oil, mix together with the milk and then beat into a batter. Cover the bowl and refrigerate.

Next, make the coleslaw by combining the red and white cabbage in a large bowl with the onion. Tip in the lemon juice and season with black pepper. Add the mayonnaise and mix all the ingredients together well, then refrigerate.

Fill a deep saucepan with oil to *no more than one third of its capacity,* then heat it. Whilst the oil is heating, cut the onions into rings approximately 0.5cm wide and separate them so that each slice has two or three layers of onion. Using suitable tongs, carefully dip the onion rings into the batter mix, then when the oil is hot enough, deep fry the onion rings a few at a time until they are golden brown. Keep the cooked onion rings warm in the oven (150°C/gas mark 2) until all are cooked.

Serve the hot onion rings with the coleslaw.

POTATO DISHES

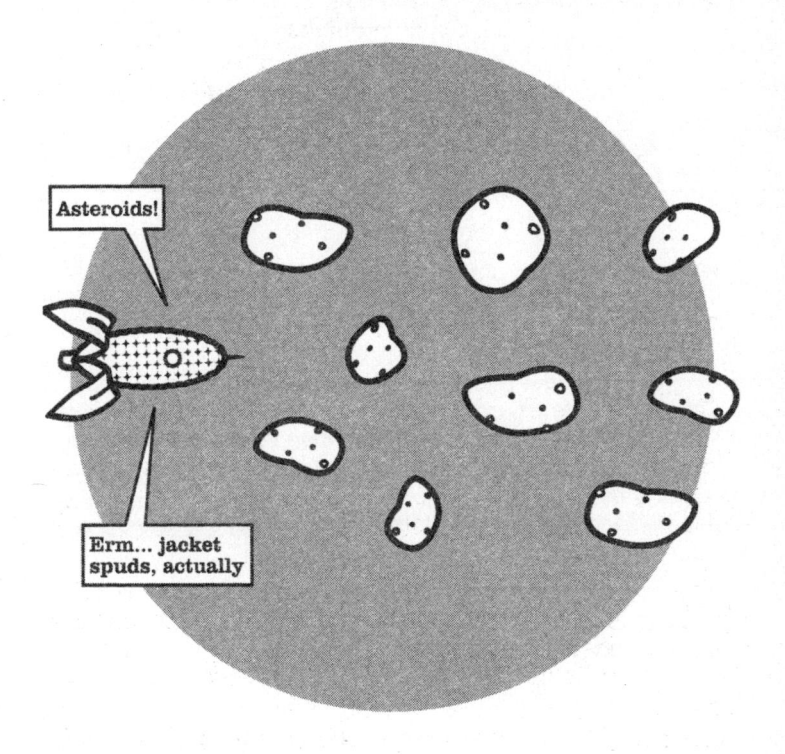

Baked Potato Slices

Serves 2

**2 large potatoes, scrubbed
2 tblsp oil
1 garlic clove, peeled and crushed
½ tsp paprika**

To serve:
small bag of prepared salad

Prick the potatoes, place them on a baking tray and bake in the oven at 200°C (gas mark 6) until almost cooked (about 50 minutes), then cool and cut into thick slices lengthways.

Arrange the slices on a greased ovenproof tray.

Mix the oil with the garlic and brush over the potato slices then sprinkle with the paprika.

Return to the oven for 10 more minutes. Delicious served with salad.

Leeky Potatoes

Serves 2

**2 large baking potatoes, scrubbed
olive oil
1 leek, well washed and finely sliced
200g soft cream cheese
salt and pepper**

Prick the potatoes, drizzle them with olive oil, place on a baking tray and bake in the oven at 200°C (gas mark 6) until soft – approximately 1 hour. (To cook faster, start the potatoes in a microwave for approximately 10 minutes on high, then transfer to the oven to crisp the skins for about 35–40 minutes.)

When the potatoes are almost ready, fry the leek in olive oil until softened and turning brown. Reduce the heat and slowly mix in the cream cheese and season to taste.

Remove the potatoes from the oven, slash the tops and push up the centres. Spoon the cheese mixture over the potatoes and serve whilst hot.

Potato Skins with Soured Cream Dip

Serves 4

**8 large baking potatoes, scrubbed
150ml soured cream
1 tsp chopped fresh chives
salt and pepper
oil for frying**

Prick the potatoes in several places, then place them on a baking tray and bake in the oven at 200°C (gas mark 6) for approximately 1 hour, or until tender.

Mix the soured cream and chives together, season and place in a bowl in the fridge to chill.

Cut the potatoes in half lengthways, then in half again and scoop out most of the flesh, leaving a 0.5cm layer next to the skin. (The potato flesh can be mashed with a little milk and butter and served as an accompaniment to another meal.)

Heat some oil in a large frying pan and fry the potato skins until golden, then drain on kitchen paper and serve with the dip.

Potato and Pea Omelette

Serves 1

**2 tblsp olive oil
150g red-skinned potatoes, unpeeled and cut into 0.25cm thick slices
½ red onion, peeled and chopped
2 eggs
salt and pepper
60g frozen peas**

Heat 1 tblsp of the oil in a frying pan and fry the potato slices until beginning to turn golden and just tender. Add the onion to the pan and cook for a further 5 minutes.

Beat the eggs together in a large bowl and season well. Add the potatoes and onions to the egg mixture, carefully so that the potatoes don't break up. Stir in the frozen peas.

Put the remaining oil in the frying pan and add the egg mixture, spreading the potatoes out evenly. Fry gently until almost set.

Heat the grill to high, then grill the omelette for 5–7 minutes until golden and set. Cut into wedges and serve.

Bubble and Squeak

Serves 4

**6 tblsp oil
1 onion, peeled and finely chopped
450g potatoes, mashed
225g cooked cabbage or Brussels sprouts, finely chopped
salt and pepper**

Heat half the oil in a large non-stick frying pan and cook the onion until soft.

Mix the potatoes and cabbage or sprouts together in a bowl and season to taste.

Add the vegetables to the frying pan, mix well with the onion then press the mixture evenly into the base of the pan.

Cook over a moderate heat for a few minutes until browned on the underside.

Place the pan under a hot grill, making sure the handle is not under the heat, and cook until the top of the mixture is browned. Serve hot, cut into wedges.

Coconut Potato Bake with Green Vegetables

Serves 4

**small amount of melted butter
750g baby potatoes, scrubbed and sliced
1 red onion, peeled and sliced
1 x 400ml can of coconut milk
284ml soured cream
1 tsp garam masala
salt and pepper
1 head of broccoli, broken into florets
200g frozen peas**

Preheat the oven to 200°C (gas mark 6).

Grease an ovenproof dish with butter and layer the potato slices and onion slices over the base.

Mix the coconut milk, soured cream, and garam masala together in a bowl, and season well. Pour this over the potato layers and cook in the hot oven for 1 hour until the potatoes are cooked and golden on top.

About 10 minutes from the end of cooking time, cook the broccoli in boiling water in a saucepan (adding a large pinch of salt) for 5 minutes then add the frozen peas to the pan and cook for a further 5 minutes or until the broccoli is *al dente*.
Serve together.

Tomato and Potato Bake

Serves 3–4

**350g medium potatoes, scrubbed and quartered
350g tomatoes
4–5 tblsp olive oil
150g feta cheese, crumbled
salt and pepper**

***To serve:*
French stick
butter**

Heat the oven to 190°C (gas mark 5).

Place the potatoes in a large saucepan of cold water, bring to the boil and cook for about 10 minutes until just tender, drain and allow to cool. Slice the tomatoes, then slice the potatoes thinly.

Brush the oil over the base and sides of an ovenproof dish and cover the bottom with a layer of half the potato slices. Then cover with half the feta cheese, season well, drizzle with oil and add a layer of half the tomato slices. Repeat the layers, finishing with tomatoes on the top.

Bake in the preheated oven for approximately 50 minutes until lightly browned on top. Serve with slices of warm French stick and butter.

Wedges N Eggs

Makes 2 generous helpings

**750g potatoes, washed and cut into wedges
olive oil for cooking
1 garlic clove, peeled and crushed
250g cherry tomatoes
6 spring onions, trimmed and chopped
salt and pepper
1 tsp paprika
4 medium eggs**

Place the potato wedges in an oven tin, drizzle with olive oil and stir in the garlic, making sure the wedges are well coated with oil. Cook in the oven at 200°C (gas mark 6) for 25 minutes.

Remove from the oven and add the cherry tomatoes and spring onions to the tin. Season and stir to ensure the vegetables are well coated. Sprinkle with paprika and cook for a further 10 minutes until the potatoes are crispy.

Break the eggs into separate cups carefully to avoid breaking the yolks.

Remove the potato mixture from the oven and make four gaps in the wedges. Carefully pour an egg into each gap, season and return to the oven for a further 5 minutes or until the eggs are just cooked.

Stuffed Baked Potatoes

Serves 4

**4 large baking potatoes, scrubbed
1 leek, well washed and thinly sliced
butter for frying
1 tblsp frozen peas
1 tblsp canned sweetcorn
½ sachet cheese sauce mix
milk, to make up the sauce
75g Cheddar cheese, grated**

Prick the potatoes in several places, then place on a baking tray and bake in the oven at 200°C (gas mark 6), until tender (about 45 minutes to 1 hour).

Meanwhile, fry the leek in some butter in a frying pan until softened (about 6–8 minutes).

When the potatoes are cooked, cut in half and carefully scoop out the centre, without damaging the skins. Mash the potato in a bowl and add the leek, peas and sweetcorn.

Make up the cheese sauce mix then add to the filling mixture, stirring thoroughly. Fill the potato skins with the mixture and place in a baking dish and cover with the grated cheese.

Return to the oven for approximately 15 minutes and cook until the tops are golden.

Feta and Potato Cakes

Serves 4

**500g potatoes, peeled
120g feta cheese
4 spring onions, trimmed and chopped
1 tblsp lemon juice
3 tsp chopped dill
1 large beaten egg
salt and pepper
small amount of flour
oil for cooking**

Cut the potatoes into small pieces, boil them for approximately 10 minutes in a saucepan, drain well, then mash without milk or butter.

Crumble the feta cheese and add to the potatoes with the onions, lemon juice, dill and beaten egg. Season lightly then chill in the fridge for 1 hour.

With floured hands, form the mixture into balls, then flatten them slightly into cakes and dust lightly with more flour.

Heat some oil in a large frying pan and cook the cakes in batches until golden brown, turning to ensure the cakes are browned on both sides. Keep the cooked cakes warm in the oven at 160°C (gas mark 3). When all the cakes are cooked, serve straight away.

Curried Jackets

Serves 2

**2 large baking potatoes
olive oil
1 onion, peeled and chopped
large knob of butter
1 tsp ground coriander
1 tsp ground cumin
1 tsp ground turmeric
1 garlic clove, peeled and crushed**

To serve:
natural yoghurt

Rub the potato skins with a little olive oil, prick them in several places, then bake on a baking tray in the oven at 200°C (gas mark 6) for about 1 hour, until cooked.

Cool a little, then cut in half and scoop the flesh from the centre of the potatoes, chopping it roughly. Put the skins back into the oven to crisp and keep warm.

Heat some olive oil in a frying pan and cook the onion until softened. Add the butter to the pan with the potato flesh, herbs and garlic and cook gently for a few minutes.

Fill the potato skins with the mixture and return to the oven to cook for about 10 more minutes until well warmed through. Remove from the oven and serve each potato with a spoonful of natural yoghurt on top.

Egg and Potato Mornay

Serves 2

450g potatoes, peeled
25g cheese, grated
25g butter
2 tblsp milk
4 hard-boiled eggs, peeled and halved

For the sauce:
50g butter
25g flour
250ml milk
½ tsp English mustard (optional)
100g cheese, grated
salt and pepper

Cut the potatoes into small pieces and boil for approximately 10 minutes in a saucepan. When cooked, mash with the cheese, butter and a little milk, mixing well together.

Cover the base of an ovenproof dish with the potato mixture then arrange the halved eggs on top.

Next, make the sauce as follows:

Put the butter in a saucepan with the flour, milk, mustard, 75g of cheese and season. Heat over a low heat, stirring constantly with a wooden spoon, until the sauce is smooth and thickened. Pour the sauce over the eggs and potatoes, then sprinkle the remaining cheese on top. Place under a hot grill until golden.

Baked Sweet Potatoes with Green Salad

Serves 4

4 sweet potatoes, skins scrubbed
melted butter
230g bag of mixed salad leaves
½ cucumber, chopped
1 small green pepper, de-seeded and sliced
salt and pepper
olive oil
2 tblsp chopped chives
4 tblsp soured cream

Preheat the oven to 200°C (gas mark 6).

Cut a cross in the flattest side of each potato with a sharp knife. Coat the potato skins with melted butter, place on a baking tray and cook in the preheated oven for 30 minutes or until tender. (Alternatively, you can begin by microwaving the potatoes for approximately 10 minutes on high, to reduce the time in the oven to about 20 minutes.)

Whilst the potatoes are cooking, mix the salad leaves, cucumber and pepper together in a salad bowl, season and drizzle with a little olive oil.

Remove the potatoes from the oven and gently squeeze the flesh. Mix the chives with the soured cream. Place the potatoes in a warmed dish and top with the soured cream mixture. Serve straight away with salad.

Rösti with Poached Egg and Green Beans

Serves 2

**2 medium potatoes, peeled
1 small onion, peeled
oil for cooking
100g green beans, topped and tailed
2 eggs
salt and freshly ground black pepper**

Grate the potatoes and onion into a bowl and combine well together, squeezing out as much moisture as possible.

Heat some oil in a non-stick frying pan and cook half the potato mixture for about 5 minutes, flattening it into the base of the pan. Turn this potato rösti over carefully and cook the other side until browned. Transfer to a non-stick baking sheet and keep warm in the oven (150°C/gas mark 2) whilst you cook the other rösti.

Meanwhile, cook the green beans in salted boiling water in a saucepan until just tender (about 8 minutes).

Break the two eggs carefully into a large saucepan of boiling water, and poach for approximately 5 minutes.

To serve, transfer the rösti to two plates, arrange the green beans over, and top with a poached egg, seasoning to taste.

Rösti can be made in advance and frozen, wrapped in greaseproof paper. When required, defrost it then remove the greaseproof paper and heat in the oven at 200°C (gas mark 6) for 8–10 minutes on a non-stick baking tray.

Cheese and Onion Jackets with Tomato Salad

Serves 2

2 baking potatoes, scrubbed
melted butter
100g cheese, grated
1 large onion, peeled and finely chopped
milk
salt and pepper
¼ iceberg lettuce, shredded
2 large tomatoes, sliced
6 sun-dried tomatoes, chopped (optional)
balsamic vinegar

Prick the potatoes in several places, rub their skins with melted butter, place them on a baking tray then bake in the oven at 200°C (gas mark 6), for about 1 hour, until just tender.

Remove from the oven and allow to cool for a few minutes. Carefully scoop out the potato flesh and place it in a bowl, leaving a 0.25cm border against the skin. Return the potato skins to the oven to crisp.

Add the cheese and onion to the potato mixture, together with a little milk and butter, then mash together and season well. Return the potato mixture to the skins and return to the oven for approximately 10 more minutes, or until the filling starts to brown.

Meanwhile, on a large serving plate arrange the lettuce with the tomato slices and sun-dried tomatoes on top, season and drizzle with a small amount of balsamic vinegar. Serve together.

Parsnip and Potato Pieces with Red Salad

Serves 4

2 tblsp olive oil
1 garlic clove, peeled and crushed
1 tsp mild curry powder
1 tsp dried coriander
2 medium potatoes
200g frozen parsnips

For the red salad:
120g red salad leaves – a mixture of radicchio and lollo rosso
1 red apple
lemon juice
handful of red seedless grapes, halved
200g beetroot, sliced
balsamic vinegar

To serve:
selection of fresh dips

Mix the olive oil with the garlic, curry powder and coriander in a small bowl and pour into a large baking tin.

Scrub the potato skins then cut into wedges and add to the baking tin, turning the potatoes to ensure they are thoroughly coated with the oil.

Cook at 200°C (gas mark 6), for 10 minutes, then add the frozen parsnips, coat them with oil and continue to cook for a further 30 minutes.

Meanwhile, wash the lettuce, shake off excess water then arrange the leaves on a large plate. Core and chop the apple into cubes and sprinkle with lemon juice to prevent browning. Just before the end of the cooking time, arrange the apple pieces, grapes and beetroot slices on the bed of lettuce and pour over a little balsamic vinegar. Serve the potato and parsnips hot with the red salad and dips.

PASTA DISHES

Linguine with Lemon Sauce

Serves 4

400g fresh linguine (spaghetti can also be used)
270ml single cream
80g Parmesan, grated
rind of 1 lemon, finely grated
75g chopped walnuts
salt and freshly ground black pepper

Cook the linguine in boiling water according to the packet instructions.

Pour the cream into a saucepan and bring to the boil, stirring. Stir in the Parmesan and lemon rind. Drain the cooked linguine, mix with the lemon sauce, and then stir in half the walnuts.

Season with salt and freshly ground black pepper, garnish with the remaining walnuts and serve.

Tuna Tagliatelle

Makes 2 large portions

oil for cooking
250g button mushrooms, quartered
375g fresh tagliatelle
1 x small can of tuna chunks, drained
3 tblsp fresh parsley, chopped
200ml half-fat crème fraîche
juice of half a lemon
salt and pepper

Heat some oil in a frying pan and cook the mushrooms until beginning to brown.

Meanwhile, cook the tagliatelle according to the packet instructions.

Stir the tuna, parsley, crème fraîche and lemon juice into the mushrooms and season well. Drain the pasta and toss with the sauce. Serve immediately.

Tagliatelle and Cider Mushrooms

Serves 2

20g butter
1 large leek, well washed and finely sliced
160g button mushrooms
200g tagliatelle
200ml dry cider
2 tblsp wholegrain mustard
100ml double cream

Heat the butter in a frying pan and fry the leek until soft, add the mushrooms and cook for further few minutes.

Meanwhile, cook the tagliatelle in a large saucepan of boiling water according to the packet instructions.

Add the cider and mustard to the leek and mushrooms; simmer until the liquid is slightly reduced. Slowly stir in the cream and simmer for 2 minutes.

Arrange the cooked tagliatelle in the pasta dish and pour the mushroom mixture over it. Serve immediately.

Tagliatelle with Herby Green Sauce

Serves 4

**300g broccoli, cut into small florets
2 onions, peeled and chopped
oil for cooking
400g full-fat cream cheese with garlic and herbs
250ml milk
350g fresh tagliatelle with herbs
2 tblsp pine nuts (optional)**

Boil the broccoli in salted water for 5 minutes in a saucepan then drain well.

Fry the onions in some oil in a frying pan until beginning to brown. Next, heat the cream cheese and milk together in a saucepan and stir constantly. Add the broccoli and onions to the sauce, mixing well together.

Meanwhile, cook the tagliatelle according to the packet instructions until *al dente*. Drain the pasta well and divide between warmed serving dishes. Spoon the sauce over the top then sprinkle with pine nuts.

Tagliatelle with Blue Cheese Sauce and Crispy Onions

Serves 4

**3 onions, peeled and finely chopped
oil for cooking
375g fresh tagliatelle
1 tblsp cornflour
500ml milk
50g crumbled blue cheese mixed with 50g grated Cheddar
salt and pepper**

Fry the onions in some oil in a frying pan until crispy.

Cook the tagliatelle according to the packet instructions.

Put the cornflour in a saucepan and stir in the milk then slowly heat the pan and add the cheese. Bring the mixture to the boil, stirring constantly. Simmer for 2 minutes then season to taste.

Serve the sauce on a bed of tagliatelle, garnished with the crispy onions.

Mediterranean Spaghetti

Serves 4

**300g spaghetti
3 tblsp olive oil
500g courgettes, halved lengthways and then sliced
2 garlic cloves, peeled and crushed
6 tomatoes, chopped
juice and zest of 1 lemon, finely grated
3 tblsp water
140g Brie, chopped
salt and pepper**

Cook the spaghetti according to the packet instructions.

Heat the oil in a large saucepan, then fry the courgettes and garlic together until softened. Add the tomatoes, lemon zest and water and cook for 5 minutes or until the tomatoes begin to soften. Remove the mixture from the heat and stir in the Brie so it just starts to melt. Season and add the lemon juice.

Drain the spaghetti and add to the tomato sauce. Toss well together and serve in warmed individual bowls.

Pasta Pronto!

Serves 3

**250g pasta (penne is good for this recipe)
1 tblsp olive oil
6 spring onions, trimmed and chopped
8 ripe tomatoes, chopped
1 tsp balsamic vinegar
6 fresh basil leaves, torn
salt and pepper
small tub of ricotta cheese**

To serve:
Parmesan shavings

Cook the pasta according to the packet instructions.

Warm the oil in a large saucepan and add the onions, tomatoes and balsamic vinegar. Cook until tender (about 5–7 minutes).

Remove from the heat and stir in the basil and season to taste. Stir in the ricotta cheese and mix with the hot drained pasta. Serve immediately with some Parmesan shavings.

Hot Pasta Salad

Serves 4

**300g pasta shapes
250g cherry tomatoes, roughly chopped
1 yellow pepper, de-seeded and chopped
handful of pitted black olives, halved
½ cucumber, sliced into thin strips with a potato peeler
4 tblsp fresh basil leaves, shredded (optional)
1 garlic clove, peeled and crushed
4 tblsp lemon juice
2 tblsp olive oil
salt and pepper**

Cook the pasta in boiling water according to the packet instructions.

In a large bowl, mix together the tomatoes, pepper, olives, cucumber, basil and garlic. Drain the pasta well and mix with the tomato mixture. Transfer to pasta dishes and drizzle with the lemon juice and olive oil, then season and serve.

This is a tasty pasta dish with a delicious no-cook sauce.

Nutty Tortellini

Serves 3–4

**250g cheese tortellini
30g butter
50g pine nuts
50g mixed chopped nuts, unsalted
1 tblsp fresh parsley, chopped
1 tblsp fresh thyme, chopped
salt and pepper
50g ricotta cheese
2 tblsp single cream**

To serve:
squirt of lemon juice

Cook the pasta according to the packet instructions until *al dente*, then drain.

Melt the butter in a frying pan and cook the nuts until golden, then add the parsley and thyme and season well. Beat together the ricotta and the cream. Fold the nut mixture into the cream and then into the pasta. Spoon into individual pasta bowls and squirt with a little lemon juice to serve.

Mushroom and Pine Nut Pasta

Serves 4–6

**400g penne pasta
270g jar of sun-dried tomatoes in olive oil
400g button mushrooms
2 garlic cloves, peeled and crushed
125ml single cream
2 tblsp shredded fresh basil
salt and pepper
2 tblsp pine nuts**

Cook the pasta in boiling water according to the packet instructions until *al dente*, then drain.

Drain the tomatoes and chop, keeping the oil. Add 1 tblsp of sun-dried tomato oil to a wok and heat. Stir fry the mushrooms for a couple of minutes, adding more oil as necessary. Add the sun-dried tomatoes and garlic to the wok, then remove from the heat and slowly add the cream. Cook for 5 minutes. Stir in the basil and pasta and season well, heat thoroughly.

Serve in warmed pasta dishes with the pine nuts sprinkled over the top.

Penne Pasta with Melted Brie

Serves 4

275g penne pasta
2 tblsp olive oil
1 large onion, peeled and chopped
550g tomatoes, chopped
2 garlic cloves, peeled and crushed
25g butter
salt and pepper
3 tblsp water
150g Brie, sliced

To garnish:
6–8 fresh basil leaves, torn

Cook the pasta according to the packet instructions.

Meanwhile, heat the oil and fry the onion in a large wok until soft. Add the tomatoes, garlic and butter and season well. Let the sauce simmer for a few minutes until the tomatoes are soft, then add 3 tblsp water and stir thoroughly.

Drain the pasta and transfer to the wok. Toss well together over a gentle heat. Stir the Brie gently into the pasta then spoon into warmed individual pasta dishes. Garnish with the basil leaves and serve.

Red Pepper Pasta

Serves 4

1 onion, peeled and sliced
1 garlic clove, peeled and crushed
1 courgette, sliced
2 red peppers, de-seeded and cut into strips
oil to cook
2 x 400g cans of chopped tomatoes
2 tblsp chopped sun-dried tomatoes
salt and pepper
250g fresh pasta
225g fresh breadcrumbs

To serve:
ciabatta bread

Fry the onion and garlic, courgette and peppers together in oil in a large saucepan and cook until softened, stirring occasionally. Add the canned and sun-dried tomatoes to the pan then season. Cover and cook until the liquid is reduced and thickened.

Meanwhile, cook the pasta according to the packet instructions until *al dente*. Drain and mix with the sauce.

Put the mixture in a shallow ovenproof dish and sprinkle with the breadcrumbs. Place under a hot grill until brown. This dish goes well with warmed ciabatta bread.

Pasta with Aubergine and Ricotta

Serves 4–6

4 tblsp olive oil
2 x 400g cans of chopped tomatoes
3 tblsp chopped fresh basil
salt and pepper
1 medium aubergine
150ml sunflower oil
500g pasta (penne is good)
250g ricotta cheese
50g Parmesan, freshly grated

Heat the olive oil in a saucepan then carefully add the canned tomatoes and cover with the lid. Cook for a few minutes then add the basil and season. Cook until reduced by one third (about 10 minutes), then remove from the heat.

Slice the aubergine into rounds then cut the rounds in half. Heat the sunflower oil in a shallow frying pan and cook the aubergine pieces a few at a time, remove them with a slotted spoon and drain on kitchen paper.

Cook the pasta in boiling water according to the packet instructions and reheat the tomato mixture. When the pasta is cooked, drain and tip into a large warmed bowl. Add the tomato mixture, crumbled ricotta and half the Parmesan, mixing well.

Spoon the pasta mixture into pasta dishes and top with the reheated aubergine slices. Sprinkle with the remaining Parmesan and serve immediately.

Pasta Gratin with Red Cheese

Serves 2

**2 eggs
110g pasta shells
1 onion, peeled and finely chopped
1 red pepper, de-seeded and finely chopped
45g butter
25g plain flour
215ml mixture of half milk, half cream
1 tsp English mustard
100g Red Leicester cheese, grated
salt and pepper
30g sun-dried tomatoes in oil, chopped
1 tblsp chopped chives
1 slice of bread, made into breadcrumbs**

To serve:
bag of prepared rocket leaves

Boil the eggs for about 7 minutes in a saucepan, then set aside to cool. Meanwhile, cook the pasta according to the packet instructions.

When the eggs are cold, peel and cut into quarters. Fry the onion and pepper together in the butter in a frying pan. Add the flour, milk mixture and mustard, stirring constantly over a gentle heat until smooth. Next, add half the grated cheese, and season well. Stir the chopped sun-dried tomatoes and chives into the cheese sauce.

Drain the pasta and place in an ovenproof dish. Pour the sauce over the top and mix well together. Gently press the egg quarters into the pasta mixture. Mix the remaining cheese with the breadcrumbs, sprinkle over the top and grill until golden brown. Serve with the rocket leaves.

MAIN COURSES

Savoury Rice Filled Peppers

Serves 4

**1 pack of savoury rice
(sweet and sour or curry flavour works well)
4 yellow peppers
2 tomatoes, sliced
125g cheese, grated**

Cook the rice according to the packet instructions, then drain.

Halve the peppers and remove the seeds. Divide the cooked rice between the peppers and top with the tomato slices. Arrange the grated cheese over the top, then carefully put the peppers into an ovenproof dish with a little water in the bottom.

Cook for approximately 30 minutes at 200°C (gas mark 6), or until the pepper skins are soft and the cheese is golden.

Pasta Stuffed Peppers

Serves 4

**4 red peppers
1 onion, peeled and chopped
1 garlic clove, peeled and crushed
2 tsp olive oil
1 x 400g can of tomatoes
275g pasta shapes
100g fresh breadcrumbs**

Cut the tops off the peppers and carefully remove the seeds from inside. Cut a thin sliver from the bottom of each pepper so that it stands upright.

Fry the onion and garlic together in the olive oil in a frying pan, then add the tomatoes and simmer gently for a few minutes.

Meanwhile, cook the pasta in boiling water according to the packet instructions until *al dente*. Drain the pasta well, then stir into the tomato sauce and spoon into the peppers. Carefully stand the peppers in an ovenproof dish, then top with the breadcrumbs. Pour a little boiling water into the base of the dish, around the peppers.

Bake in the oven at 200°C (gas mark 6), for about 30 minutes, or until the peppers are soft.

Cheese Pudding

Serves 2

**250ml milk
30g fresh breadcrumbs
125g Cheddar cheese, grated
2 eggs
1 tsp English mustard
salt and pepper**

Bring the milk to the boil in a saucepan. Place the breadcrumbs in a bowl and pour the milk over, then stir in the cheese.

In a separate bowl, beat the eggs and then add the mustard. Mix in the milk and breadcrumbs and season well.

Butter a shallow ovenproof dish and pour in the cheese pudding mixture. Bake at 180°C (gas mark 4) for about 30 minutes until lightly set and golden.

Broccoli Bake

Serves 2

**1 small head of broccoli, broken into florets
40g butter
25g plain flour
250ml milk
1 tsp English mustard
100g cheese, grated
salt and pepper**

Boil the broccoli in a saucepan until tender (about 5 minutes), drain, then arrange in an ovenproof dish.

Make the cheese sauce: put the butter, flour, milk, mustard and half the grated cheese into a small saucepan and heat, stirring constantly to prevent sticking. When mixed into a smooth sauce, pour over the broccoli, season then sprinkle the remaining cheese over the top.

Cook in the oven at 200°C (gas mark 6) for approximately 30 minutes, or until the topping is golden.

Mushroom Stroganoff

Serves 4

olive oil to cook
500g mixed mushrooms, sliced
1 garlic clove, peeled and chopped
1 bunch of spring onions, trimmed and chopped
250ml vegetable stock
150ml double cream
2 tblsp brandy (optional)
salt and pepper

To serve:
250g long grain rice

Heat some oil in a large frying pan or wok, and stir fry the mushrooms with the garlic and spring onions for approximately 5 minutes. Stir in the vegetable stock then add the cream and brandy. Season to taste, stir the mixture for a further 5 minutes until warmed thoroughly.

Meanwhile, cook the rice according to the packet instructions. Serve the stroganoff on a bed of rice.

Sweetcorn Fritters

Serves 2

**200g canned sweetcorn
200g cooked potatoes, mashed without butter or milk
1 egg white
1 tblsp fresh parsley, chopped
1 tsp mustard
salt and pepper
flour for shaping
oil for cooking**

Take care: sweetcorn tends to spit when fried! It is a good idea to use a splash guard if you have one, when making the fritters.

Mix the sweetcorn with mashed potatoes in a bowl. Beat the egg white in another bowl until frothy then stir into the potato mixture, and add the parsley, mustard, salt and pepper.

With floured hands, form the mixture into small fritter shapes and fry in some heated oil in a shallow non-stick frying pan, turning carefully to brown on both sides.

Vegetable Rice Bake

Serves 2

**125g long grain brown rice
2 vegetable stock cubes
500g fresh seasonal vegetables (selection of either: carrots/broccoli/swede; or baby corn/mange-tout/courgette), cut into similar sizes
100g cheese, grated
salt and pepper
25g butter**

Cook the rice according to the packet instructions then drain well.

Dissolve the stock cubes in 1 litre of boiling water.

Boil the vegetables for approximately 10 minutes, depending on size, until just tender then mix the cooked vegetables with the rice and put in a shallow ovenproof dish, and pour the stock over. Sprinkle with the grated cheese, season and dot with butter.

Bake in the oven at 200°C (gas mark 6) until the mixture is hot and the cheese is bubbling – about 20–25 minutes.

Savoury Tuna Rice

Serves 2

**175g long grain rice
oil for stir frying
1 onion, peeled and chopped
100g frozen peas
1 x small can of flaked tuna, drained
6 sun-dried tomatoes, chopped
2 tblsp soy sauce**

Cook the rice according to the packet instructions, then leave to cool.

Heat some oil in a non-stick wok and fry the onion for 5 minutes, add the rice then stir fry with the peas for a few minutes, stirring continually to prevent sticking. Add the tuna and sun-dried tomatoes and heat for a further 2–3 minutes, add the soy sauce and stir through well.

Can be eaten hot or cold. *However, if not eaten straight away, make sure the rice is cooled as quickly as possible and kept in the fridge for no more than one day before eating. Bacteria which causes food poisoning grows on cooked rice left at room temperature.*

Crispy Mushroom Bake

Serves 2

**90g fresh breadcrumbs
75g chopped nuts
margarine for cooking
1 onion, peeled and chopped
150g mushrooms, sliced
200g canned tomatoes, chopped
1 garlic clove, peeled and crushed
1 tsp dried mixed herbs
salt and pepper**

Mix the breadcrumbs and nuts together and fry in melted margarine in a frying pan until golden, then set aside.

Melt some more margarine in a saucepan and fry the onion until soft, add the mushrooms and cook gently. Add the tomatoes, garlic and herbs and cook for a further 5 minutes, season well.

Put the mushroom mixture in a shallow ovenproof dish and cover with a layer of breadcrumbs and nuts. Bake in the oven at 190°C (gas mark 5) for about 20 minutes, or until golden and crisp. Serve piping hot.

Crunchy Topped Vegetable Casserole

Serves 2

110g carrots, peeled and sliced
1 onion, peeled and sliced
1 stick of celery, sliced
125g potatoes, peeled and sliced
25g swede, peeled and sliced
300ml vegetable stock
salt and pepper
125g canned butter beans
30g frozen peas
75g fresh breadcrumbs and grated cheese, mixed together

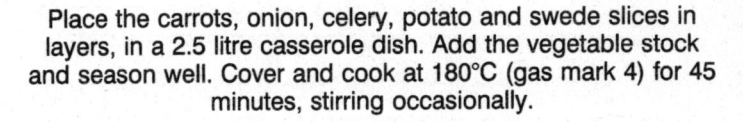

Place the carrots, onion, celery, potato and swede slices in layers, in a 2.5 litre casserole dish. Add the vegetable stock and season well. Cover and cook at 180°C (gas mark 4) for 45 minutes, stirring occasionally.

Remove from the oven and add the beans and peas to the casserole, stirring well. Top the casserole with the breadcrumbs and cheese, then continue to bake for a further 15 minutes.

Vegetarian Chilli

Serves 4

**oil for cooking
1 large onion, peeled and sliced
1 garlic clove, peeled and crushed
1 x 400g can of tomatoes
1 x 400g can of red kidney beans, drained
1 red pepper, de-seeded and chopped
1 courgette, sliced
2 carrots, finely chopped
6 mushrooms, chopped
1 tsp chilli powder – vary amount according to taste
300ml vegetable stock
½ tblsp tomato puree**

To serve:
280g long grain rice

In a wok, fry in some oil the onion with the garlic until soft. Add the other ingredients and simmer gently for 30 minutes, stirring from time to time to prevent sticking.

Towards the end of cooking time, cook the rice according to the packet instructions.

Serve the chilli on a bed of rice.

Sweet and Sour Noodles

Serves 4

**1 red, 1 green and 1 yellow pepper, de-seeded, cut into rings then halved
1 garlic clove, peeled and crushed
2 tblsp chopped sun-dried tomatoes
1 tblsp wholegrain mustard
grated rind and juice of 1 lime
2 tblsp fresh coriander, chopped
1 tblsp olive oil
2 tsp soy sauce
salt and pepper
200g egg noodles**

Boil the pepper slices in a saucepan of water until softened (about 6 minutes), then drain well.

Mix the garlic, sun-dried tomatoes, mustard, lime, coriander, olive oil and soy sauce together in a bowl and season well.

Cook the noodles according to the packet instructions, then drain and return to the pan. Add the peppers and dressing, and toss well together. Divide between warmed bowls and serve.

Baked Beetroot

Serves 4

40g butter
210g cooked beetroot, sliced*
200g cheese, grated
284ml double cream
salt and pepper
fresh breadcrumbs (approximately 2 slices)

Dot half the butter over the base of four shallow ovenproof dishes and cover with a layer of beetroot. Cover with the grated cheese then pour the cream over the top. Season well then cover with the fresh breadcrumbs.

Dot the breadcrumbs with the remaining butter then bake in the oven at 180°C (gas mark 4) for approximately 10 minutes until the topping is golden. Alternatively, you can heat under a hot grill, ensuring the dish is well heated through.

*You can either use fresh beetroot, boiled for about 1 hour until tender (do not allow the pan to boil dry), then peeled, or, for ease, use pre-packed cooked beetroot (not beetroot in vinegar as the flavour is too strong).

Artichoke Bake

Serves 4

**1 onion, peeled and finely chopped
1 green pepper, de-seeded and finely chopped
1 red pepper, de-seeded and finely chopped
1 yellow pepper, de-seeded and finely chopped
margarine for frying
1 x 400g can of artichoke hearts
50g Edam cheese, grated
50g fresh breadcrumbs
1 tsp paprika
4 cherry tomatoes, sliced**

Preheat the oven to 200°C (gas mark 6).

In a frying pan, fry the onion and peppers together in some margarine for 5 minutes.

Drain the artichokes and slice them, then divide them between four shallow greased ovenproof dishes. Spread the pepper mixture over the top. Mix the cheese and breadcrumbs together in a bowl and stir in the paprika. Cover each dish with the cheese mixture, then lay the tomato slices along the centre.

Bake the dishes in the preheated oven for 20–25 minutes, or until hot and bubbling on the top.

Mexican Re-Fried Beans

Serves 4

2 tblsp vegetable oil
1 onion, peeled and finely chopped
1 garlic clove, peeled and crushed
1 green chilli, de-seeded and finely chopped*
2 x 400g cans of red kidney beans
150ml water

To serve:
4 tomatoes, roughly chopped
½ cucumber, cut into wedges
soured cream
tortilla chips

Heat the oil in a frying pan and fry the onion, garlic and chilli together until the onion is softened.

Drain and rinse the kidney beans then mash them in a bowl and add to the frying pan with 150ml water, stir well. Cook gently for about 5 minutes, stirring constantly and adding more water if the beans start to stick.

Serve hot with the tomato and cucumber wedges, soured cream and tortilla chips.

Wash hands after touching chillies or wear rubber gloves as chillies can sting eyes or sensitive skin.

Aubergine and Mozzarella Grills

Serves 2

**wooden skewers, broken in half
1 large aubergine, cut lengthways into 0.5cm slices
olive oil to cook
sun-dried tomato paste
150g mozzarella, thinly sliced
bunch of fresh basil leaves**

To serve:
crusty bread

Soak the skewers in water for at least half an hour, to prevent burning in the oven. Preheat the oven to 160°C (gas mark 3).

Brush the aubergine slices with plenty of oil and grill on each side until softened and beginning to brown, adding more oil as required. Then, thinly spread some tomato paste on one side of the aubergine slices. Add the mozzarella slices and a basil leaf to each aubergine slice. Roll up the aubergine slices and secure with the skewers.

Heat in the oven until the cheese begins to soften (about 10–15 minutes). During the last few minutes of cooking put some crusty bread in the oven to warm.

Serve with the hot crusty bread.

Tomato Crumble

Serves 2

**5 tblsp olive oil
250g tomatoes, chopped
250g whole cherry tomatoes
100g goat's cheese
50g pine nuts
100g fresh breadcrumbs
50g Parmesan, grated**

Preheat the oven to 190°C (gas mark 5).

Heat 2 tblsp oil in a frying pan and fry the chopped tomatoes until softened, stirring from time to time, then add the cherry tomatoes and cook for a further 5 minutes.

Put half the tomato mixture into a 1 litre ovenproof dish and crumble half of the goat's cheese over the top, add a further layer of tomatoes and top with the remaining cheese.

Wipe the frying pan clean, then heat 3 tblsp olive oil in it and fry the pine nuts and breadcrumbs together for about 6 minutes. Scatter the breadcrumb mixture over the tomatoes and cheese, then top with the Parmesan.

Bake in the preheated oven until golden, approximately 20 minutes.

Paella

Serves 2–3

**2 tblsp vegetable oil for cooking
½ large onion, peeled and chopped
½ large red pepper, de-seeded and chopped
180g long grain rice
750ml vegetable stock
1 garlic clove, peeled and crushed
90g button mushrooms, cut into quarters
2 large tomatoes, chopped
125g canned artichoke hearts, chopped
90g mange-tout
75g canned water chestnuts, sliced
90g frozen peas
1 tsp turmeric**

Heat the oil in a wok and cook the onion and red pepper until soft. Add the rice and cook for 2–3 minutes, stirring constantly to avoid sticking. Add the stock little by little, stirring until almost absorbed. Add the garlic and continue to cook until the rice is tender.

Add the remaining ingredients, adding a little water if the mixture becomes too dry. Continue to simmer gently until all the vegetables are cooked (about 10 minutes).

Courgettes and Corn in Lemon Sauce with Spicy Couscous

Serves 2

**oil for frying
1 courgette, cut into slices approximately 0.5cm thick
½ garlic clove, peeled and crushed
8 baby corn, cut in half
200ml crème fraîche
2 tsp lemon juice
1 tblsp fresh chopped basil
salt and pepper
50g plain couscous
¼ red chilli, de-seeded and finely chopped***

Stir fry in some oil in a frying pan the courgette slices with the garlic until softened. Then add the baby corn, crème fraîche, lemon juice, basil and seasoning, and continue to cook gently.

Meanwhile, put the couscous and chilli into a saucepan and cook according to the packet instructions. Serve together.

*Wash hands after touching chillies or wear rubber gloves as chillies can sting eyes or sensitive skin.

Cheesy Leeks and Aubergines

Serves 4

**2 medium aubergines, cut into 8 slices lengthways, each approximately 0.5cm thick
olive oil for cooking
4 large leeks, trimmed, well washed and cut in half
1 tblsp Dijon mustard
6 tblsp crème fraîche
100g cheese, grated
salt and pepper**

To serve:
crusty bread and butter

Heat the grill to high. Brush the aubergine slices with olive oil and grill on both sides until softened and brown.

Cook the leeks in a saucepan of boiling water until just tender (about 10 minutes), drain and cool. Wrap each leek in an aubergine slice and lay in an ovenproof dish.

Mix the mustard, crème fraîche and cheese together in a bowl, reserving a little cheese. Season to taste and pour over the leeks and aubergines, then sprinkle the remaining cheese over the top.

Bake at 200°C (gas mark 6) for about 20 minutes, or until the top is bubbling and golden. Serve with crusty bread and butter.

Golden Aubergine Slices

Serves 2

**50g plain flour
salt and pepper
120g fresh breadcrumbs
2 eggs
1 large aubergine, cut into 1cm rounds
oil for frying**

To serve:
**shredded radicchio leaves
sweet chilli dip**

Season the flour well and pour onto a plate, put the breadcrumbs on a second plate, then beat the eggs together in a bowl.

Cover both sides of the aubergine slices in flour, then dip well in the beaten egg and coat each slice well with the breadcrumbs.

Heat some oil in a deep frying pan, then fry the aubergine slices in batches until golden brown all over. Drain them well on kitchen paper before serving.

Once cooked, aubergine slices can be kept warm in the oven (150°C/gas mark 2) until they are ready to be served. Delicious served with shredded radicchio and a sweet chilli dip.

Stir Fry Radishes with Garlic Bread

Serves 3

**1 French stick
90g soft butter
2 garlic cloves, peeled and finely chopped
1 large bunch of radishes, trimmed and sliced
1 red onion, peeled and thinly sliced
2 tblsp soured cream
1 tsp salt**

Diagonally cut the French stick into slices. Mix 75g butter in a bowl with the chopped garlic and thickly butter the cut sides of the French stick. Press the slices back together and wrap in foil.

Place on a baking sheet and cook in the oven at 200°C (gas mark 6) for approximately 10 minutes (until the bread is well warmed and crispy and the butter has melted).

Meanwhile, melt the remaining butter in a saucepan and add the radishes and red onion. Cook until tender (about 8–10 minutes), stirring from time to time. Drain off any excess liquid and stir in the soured cream. Season to taste. Serve with the hot garlic bread.

Curried Bean Bake

Serves 4

**4 medium potatoes, peeled
2 carrots, peeled
butter
½ tsp cumin
1 onion, peeled and chopped
1 x 400g can of chopped tomatoes with herbs
200g canned red kidney beans
200g canned curried beans (or baked beans with a little curry paste)
200g canned black-eyed or butter beans
1 tsp cornflour blended to a paste with a little water
salt and pepper**

Cut the potatoes and carrots into similar-sized chunks and boil in a saucepan until tender (about 8 minutes, depending on size), then mash together with a little butter and cumin.

Meanwhile, fry the onion in some butter until soft, then add the tomatoes, beans and cornflour mixture. Bring to the boil whilst stirring until the mixture thickens, season to taste. Transfer the mixture to an ovenproof dish and spread the mashed potatoes over the top and grill until starting to brown.

Chilli Mix with Potato and Carrot Mash

Serves 2

**2 large carrots, peeled
2 large potatoes, peeled
1 onion, peeled and chopped
1 green pepper, de-seeded and chopped
oil to cook
8 button mushrooms, halved
200g canned red kidney beans, rinsed
1 x 400g can of chopped tomatoes
½ tsp hot chilli powder
pinch of nutmeg
small amount of milk and butter**

Cut the carrots into chunks and boil in a saucepan for 5 minutes, then cut the potatoes into slightly larger pieces and add to the pan, reduce the heat and simmer for 8–10 minutes.

In a large frying pan cook the onion and green pepper in some oil until softened, add the mushrooms and cook for a further 5 minutes. Add the kidney beans, canned tomatoes and chilli powder and cook gently.

When the potatoes and carrots are cooked, drain and mash together with the nutmeg, milk and butter. Divide the potato mixture between two plates, making a well in the centre. Fill the centre with the chilli mix and serve.

Ratatouille with Spicy Couscous

Serves 4

**250g potatoes, peeled and sliced
1 onion, peeled and sliced
1 green pepper, de-seeded and sliced
1 yellow pepper, de-seeded and sliced
1 garlic clove, peeled and crushed
sunflower oil
1 x 400g can of tomatoes
1 tblsp soy sauce
salt and pepper**

To serve:
**200g packet of couscous
½ red chilli, de-seeded and very finely chopped*
handful of dried apricots, finely chopped**

Fry the potatoes, onion and peppers together with the garlic in hot oil in a wok for 5 minutes. Add the tomatoes, soy sauce and seasoning and bring to the boil then simmer gently for approximately 20 minutes, or until the vegetables are tender.

Put the couscous in a saucepan with the chilli and apricots and cook according to the packet instructions. Serve together.

*Wash hands after touching chillies or wear rubber gloves as chillies can sting eyes or sensitive skin.

Stuffed Aubergines with Tomato Sauce

Serves 2

**2 aubergines
75g fresh breadcrumbs
1 onion, peeled and sliced
100g mushrooms, sliced
1 tsp mixed herbs
salt and pepper
1 beaten egg
grated cheese
1 x 400g can of chopped tomatoes
dash of Tabasco sauce**

Cut the aubergines in half lengthways and scoop out the seeds and discard them. Then, scoop out the flesh and chop finely, leaving a border around the edge.

Place the breadcrumbs in a bowl with the onion, aubergine flesh, mushrooms, herbs and seasoning. Mix together then add the beaten egg. Spoon the mixture evenly into the aubergine shells, then sprinkle a little grated cheese on top. Tip the chopped tomatoes into an ovenproof dish and stir in the Tabasco sauce, then place the aubergine halves on top.

Cover and cook at 200°C (gas mark 6) for about 40 minutes. Remove the cover, then continue to cook for another 20 minutes until the topping is golden.

Tomatoes with Cheese Soufflé Filling

Serves 4

**8 large tomatoes
125ml milk
100g Stilton cheese, crumbled
2 tsp cornflour
2 eggs
salt and pepper
1 tblsp chopped tarragon**

Preheat the oven to 200°C (gas mark 6).

Cut the tops from the tomatoes and scoop out the flesh. Turn the tomatoes upside down to drain. In a saucepan, heat the milk and add the cheese, stirring well together. Add a little cold water to the cornflour and mix to a smooth paste, then add this to the pan and stir together until bubbling. Remove from the heat and allow to cool slightly.

Separate the yolks and whites of the eggs, then add the yolks to the sauce and beat well together. Whip the egg whites until forming peaks, then fold into the sauce. Season well and add the chopped tarragon. Carefully spoon the mixture into the tomatoes, then put the tomato lids on the top.

Transfer the tomatoes to a greased ovenproof dish and cook in the oven for about 15 minutes.

Savoury Rice Supper

Serves 4

**225g basmati rice
2 tblsp oil for frying
2 garlic cloves, peeled and crushed
1 onion, peeled and chopped
1 carrot, chopped
50g sweetcorn
50g frozen peas
25g cashew nuts
½ tsp ground cumin**

Wash the rice well then place in a bowl, cover with water and leave for 30 minutes.

In a wok, fry together in the oil the garlic, onion and carrot for 6–8 minutes.

Drain the rice well then add it to the wok with the sweetcorn, peas and cashew nuts and continue to cook, gently. Add the cumin and 475ml water, cover and simmer gently for about 15 minutes, until the rice is cooked and the water absorbed, checking occasionally that the rice is not sticking.

Once cooked, leave to stand, covered, for 5 minutes before serving.

Deep-Fried Brie with Kiwi

Serves 2

**400–500g Brie, cut into 2cm wedges, rind left on
1 beaten egg
shop-bought golden breadcrumbs
oil to deep fry**

To serve:
**2 kiwi fruit, peeled and cut into large chunks
green salad leaves
cranberry sauce**

Take extra care when deep-fat frying. Hot oil spits wildly and can rise up the sides of the pan very quickly.

Coat the Brie chunks in the beaten egg then roll in the golden breadcrumbs until evenly coated.

Fill a large saucepan with oil to *no more than one-third of its capacity*. Heat the oil. To test if it is hot enough, drop a small cube of bread into the oil: it should begin to bubble immediately. When hot enough lower the Brie into the pan and deep fry in batches of four for about a minute or until the breadcrumbs start to brown. Do not overcook or the cheese will melt. Remove with a heatproof slotted spoon and drain on kitchen paper in a warm dish.

When all the Brie is cooked, divide between two plates and add the kiwi chunks. Serve immediately with salad and a little cranberry sauce.

Red and Green Frittata

Serves 2

½ red onion, peeled and chopped
100g courgettes, thinly sliced
oil to cook
1 garlic clove, peeled and crushed
2 medium eggs
salt and black pepper
75g canned flageolet beans, rinsed and drained
2 tomatoes, chopped
1 tblsp fresh basil and chives, chopped
30g cheese, grated

To serve:
crusty bread and butter

Fry the onion and courgettes in a large frying pan in some hot oil with the garlic until softened.

Beat the eggs in a bowl, season then add the canned beans, fried vegetables, tomatoes, herbs and stir well together.

Wipe the frying pan clean, then heat more oil in it, tip in the mixture and fry over a gentle heat for 5 minutes or until the eggs have almost set and the underside of the frittata is golden. Sprinkle the cheese over the top then place under a hot grill until the cheese starts to bubble.

Serve warm or hot with crusty bread and butter

Creamy Cheese Pizza

Makes 1 x 25cm pizza

**3–4 tblsp tomato sauce for pizza/Bolognese
1 x 25cm prepared pizza base
1 small red onion, peeled and sliced thinly
½ yellow pepper, de-seeded and cut into small pieces
4 button mushrooms, sliced
5 cherry tomatoes, halved
100g cream cheese**

To serve:
bag of rocket leaves

Preheat the oven to 200°C (gas mark 6).

Spoon the tomato sauce over the pizza base, then top with the red onion, pepper, mushrooms and cherry tomatoes. Dot small amounts of cream cheese over the top and cook until the vegetables are soft and golden (approximately 20 minutes).

Serve with some rocket leaves.

Focaccia Pizza

Serves 2

**300g tomatoes, chopped
1 onion, peeled and chopped
1 garlic clove, peeled and crushed
2 tblsp olive oil
1 round focaccia loaf with herbs
100g mozzarella cheese, sliced
50g pitted black olives
fresh basil leaves
freshly ground black pepper**

Preheat the oven to 200°C (gas mark 6).

Mix the tomatoes, onion and garlic in a roasting tin, then drizzle with the olive oil. Roast in the oven for 15 minutes, until softened and beginning to char.

Crush the vegetable mixture with a fork. Split the loaf in half and place the two rounds on a baking tray lined with greaseproof paper. Spread the tomato mixture over the top, leaving excess fluid in the tin. Top with the mozzarella slices, olives and most of the basil.

Bake in the oven for about 10 minutes, or until the cheese has melted. Season with black pepper and serve with some basil leaves.

Roast Vegetable Pizza

Serves 2

**1 red and 1 yellow pepper, de-seeded and cut into chunks
1 courgette, sliced
olive oil
1 x 25cm ready-made pizza base or
2 smaller pizza bases
5 tblsp passata (or canned tomatoes, finely chopped)
100g button mushrooms, thinly sliced
75g grated cheese or sliced mozzarella**

To garnish:
rocket leaves

Preheat the oven to 200°C (gas mark 6).

Put the peppers and courgette on a non-stick baking tray and drizzle with a little olive oil. Roast for 15 minutes then remove from the oven. Increase the temperature to 220°C (gas mark 7).

Put the pizza base on a non-stick baking tray then spread the tomato mixture over the top. Arrange the roast vegetables and mushrooms on top of the pizza base. Sprinkle with the cheese and drizzle with a little olive oil. Bake in the oven for approximately 20 minutes, or until golden.

Garnish with some rocket leaves and serve.

Red Onion and Pepper Tarts

Makes 2 tarts

**1 sheet of frozen puff pastry, thawed
1 red onion, peeled and chopped
1 red pepper, de-seeded and chopped
oil for cooking
2 thick tomato slices
10 pitted black or green olives, chopped (optional)
salt and pepper
milk**

To serve:
balsamic vinegar

Cut two circles (diameter approximately 13cm), from the sheet of puff pastry. Score a 1cm border around the edges of the circles, then place the pastry on a lightly greased baking tray.

Fry the onion and pepper together in some oil in a frying pan until browned and soft.

Cover the pastry rounds with the mixture, avoiding the border. Top with the tomato slices and olives, then season. Brush the borders of the tarts with a little milk. Drizzle the centres of the tarts with a little olive oil and cook for 15–20 minutes at 220°C (gas mark 7), or until the pastry is golden.

To serve, add a splash of balsamic vinegar.

Tomato, Stilton and Mozzarella Tart

Serves 4

**500g vine-ripened or plum tomatoes
salt and black pepper
olive oil to cook
1 sheet frozen ready-rolled puff pastry (about 215g), thawed
100g Stilton cheese, crumbled
100g mozzarella cheese, in small pieces
1 tsp fresh thyme leaves, chopped**

To serve:
rocket leaves

Cut the tomatoes in half lengthways and place them cut-side-up in a shallow roasting tin. Season, drizzle with a little olive oil and roast at 200°C (gas mark 6), until they are shrivelled but still juicy (approximately 30 minutes). If they appear to be drying out whilst cooking, drizzle with a little more olive oil. Remove from the oven and set aside.

Unroll the pastry sheet and place on a greased baking sheet, prick all over with a fork and bake blind (i.e. without any filling) for approximately 20 minutes, until golden.

Take out of the oven and carefully turn the pastry over and cook for a further 5 minutes. Place the tomato halves over the pastry, leaving a border around the edge. Cover with the Stilton and mozzarella, add the chopped thyme leaves, and drizzle with more olive oil. Place back in the oven until the cheese has melted.

Serve immediately with some rocket leaves scattered over the surface and a light drizzling of olive oil.

Nutty Stilton Tart

Serves 6

**600g onions, peeled and sliced
oil for frying
1 tblsp balsamic vinegar
salt and pepper
1 sheet frozen ready-rolled puff pastry (about 215g), thawed
175g Stilton cheese
50g walnut pieces**

To serve:
**bag of mixed salad
mild tomato salsa**

Fry the onions in some hot oil in a frying pan until golden and softened. Add the balsamic vinegar to the pan, season, then continue to cook for a further few minutes until beginning to caramelise.

Unroll the pastry and use to line the bottom of a shallow greased baking tin. Prick the pastry all over with a fork and cook at 200°C (gas mark 6) for 20 minutes, then remove from the oven and carefully turn the pastry over. Return to the oven and cook for a further 5 minutes. Remove from the oven and cover the pastry with the onions, crumble the Stilton over the top and add the walnut pieces. Bake for about 20 minutes at 200°C (gas mark 6) until the pastry is golden and the cheese melted.

Cool for a few minutes then cut into chunks and serve with salad and a mild tomato salsa.

This recipe can be prepared the day before. When required, cook in the hot oven (200°C/gas mark 6) for 20 minutes and serve.

Pesto Mushrooms with Lemon Couscous

Serves 2

**10 medium mushrooms
small jar of pesto
10 cherry tomatoes
40ml olive oil
salt and black pepper**

To serve:
**60g plain couscous
dash of lemon juice**

Brush the mushrooms clean, remove their stalks and place the mushrooms in an ovenproof dish. Spoon some pesto into each mushroom and top each mushroom with a cherry tomato. Drizzle with a little olive oil and season with salt and black pepper.

Pour a little boiling water carefully into the base of the dish to prevent the mushrooms from sticking. Cook at 200°C (gas mark 6) for approximately 20 minutes, or until the tomatoes begin to soften. Midway through cooking, spoon some of the juice from the dish over the mushrooms to prevent them from drying out.

Cook the couscous according to the packet instructions, then divide between serving plates and drizzle with lemon juice. Make a well in the centre of the couscous and place the cooked mushrooms there. Serve immediately.

Chilli Noodles

Serves 2

1 onion, peeled and finely chopped
1 garlic clove, peeled and crushed
2 tblsp olive oil
1 aubergine, cut into cubes
50g sun-dried tomatoes, sliced
1 fresh chilli, de-seeded and finely chopped, (or ½ tsp chilli powder)*
200ml crème fraîche
250g fine egg noodles

To serve:
grated cheese

Cook the onion and garlic in the oil in a large saucepan until softened. Add the aubergine and continue to cook. Next add the sun-dried tomatoes and chilli, turn the heat to the lowest setting, cover and cook for about 10 minutes, stirring occasionally. Add the crème fraîche and cook for a further 5 minutes.

Cook the noodles in boiling water according to the packet instructions. Drain the noodles well, then stir in the aubergine mixture. Serve immediately, sprinkled with grated cheese.

*How much chilli you use will vary according to taste. Wash hands after touching chillies or wear rubber gloves as chillies can sting eyes or sensitive skin.

Chargrilled Vegetables with Rice

Serves 4

**sun-dried tomato olive oil (or olive oil and 8 chopped sun-dried tomatoes) for cooking
2 garlic cloves, peeled and crushed
2 aubergines, sliced
4 courgettes, sliced
1 red and 1 yellow pepper, de-seeded and cut into large pieces
2 red onions, peeled and sliced
12 cherry tomatoes
salt and pepper**

To serve:
**275g long grain rice
chopped chives**

Preheat the grill. Drizzle the olive oil across the base of a baking sheet or grill pan, sprinkle on the garlic and then add the vegetables, turning them to coat them thoroughly with oil and garlic. Grill until the vegetables are softened and beginning to char – you may have to grill them in batches, putting the cooked vegetables in the oven at 160°C (gas mark 3) to keep warm. Season well.

Meanwhile, cook the rice according to the packet instructions.

Serve the vegetables on a bed of rice and sprinkle with some chopped chives

---

Cheesy Zucchini

Serves 2

150ml bread sauce mix
milk
1 small onion, peeled and chopped
butter
2 courgettes
4 tblsp grated cheese
large pinch of dried mixed herbs
salt and pepper

Preheat the oven to 190°C (gas mark 5).

Make the bread sauce with the milk, according to the packet instructions. In a frying pan, fry the onion in some butter until soft, then add to the bread mixture.

Wash the courgettes, cut in half across the middle and cook in a large saucepan of boiling salted water for 5 minutes, drain and leave to cool. When cooled, cut the courgettes in half lengthways and scoop out the flesh with a sharp knife, leaving a 0.25cm shell. Chop finely and add to the bread mixture. Add the cheese and herbs to the bowl, mix well together and season. Fill the courgette shells with the mixture.

Pour a little water into the base of a shallow ovenproof dish and arrange the courgettes closely together in the dish. Bake in the preheated oven for approximately 30 minutes until golden.

Lemony Tomatoes with Rice and Bean Salad

Serves 4

**120g packet golden savoury rice
4 large tomatoes, thickly sliced
4 tblsp olive oil
2 tblsp lemon juice
1 x 400g can of red kidney beans, drained and rinsed
1 green pepper, de-seeded and very finely chopped
2 sticks celery, very finely chopped
1 red onion, peeled and very finely chopped
1 tblsp white wine vinegar
1 garlic clove, peeled and crushed
1 tsp wholegrain mustard
1 tsp chopped fresh coriander**

Cook the rice according to the instructions on the packet, then leave to cool.

Place the tomato slices on a grill pan and drizzle with 1 tblsp olive oil. Turn over so both sides are coated with oil, then drizzle with the lemon juice. Place under a hot grill and cook until the tomatoes are soft. Meanwhile, stir the beans, pepper, celery and onion into the cooled rice.

Mix the remaining olive oil, white wine vinegar, garlic and mustard together and stir into the rice salad. Arrange the warm tomato slices on a plate with the rice salad at the side. Sprinkle the salad with the fresh coriander and serve.

Meat-Free Burgers

Makes 4 burgers

**115g mushrooms, finely chopped
1 onion, peeled and finely chopped
1 small courgette, finely chopped
1 small carrot, finely chopped
oil for frying
salt and pepper
115g fresh breadcrumbs
25g nuts, finely chopped
2 tblsp chopped fresh parsley
1 tsp Marmite
½ tsp chilli powder (optional)
2 beaten eggs
flour for shaping**

Fry the vegetables together in some oil in a frying pan until the onion is just tender (about 6–8 minutes), then season.

Remove from the heat then stir in the breadcrumbs, nuts, parsley, Marmite, chilli powder (if used), and beaten egg until the mixture binds together.

With floured hands, form the mixture into four burger shapes. Chill for about 1 hour in the refrigerator.

Wipe the frying pan clean, then fry the burgers in it in a little hot oil, turning carefully, for approximately 10–15 minutes or until they are cooked through and golden brown on the outside.

Wild Rice with Roast Vegetables

Serves 4

**1 aubergine, thickly sliced
2 red onions, peeled and sliced
1 red, 1 yellow and 1 green pepper, de-seeded and cut into quarters
225g mixed mushrooms
2 small courgettes, thickly sliced
olive oil
115g long grain rice
115g wild rice**

For the dressing
**6 tblsp olive oil
2 tblsp balsamic vinegar
2 garlic cloves, peeled and crushed
salt and pepper**

Arrange the vegetables in a large baking tin, brush with some olive oil and cook in the oven at 200°C (gas mark 6) for approximately 30 minutes or until tender and well browned, turning occasionally to coat with oil.

Cook the rice according to the packet instructions and mix together.

To make the dressing – mix together the olive oil, vinegar, garlic and seasoning in a jug.

Drain the rice and toss in half the dressing. Transfer to a serving dish and arrange the vegetables on top. Pour over the remainder of the dressing and serve at once.

Spinach and Feta Muffins

Makes 6 muffins

**150g spinach leaves
1 garlic clove, peeled and crushed
2 eggs
2 egg whites
2 tblsp grated Cheddar cheese
60ml milk
salt
½ tsp cayenne pepper
70g feta cheese, cut into 18 small cubes**

To cook:
6-hole non-stick muffin tin

Preheat the oven to 200°C (gas mark 6).

Wash the spinach and place in a saucepan of boiling water with the garlic. Heat for 5 minutes until the spinach is wilted. Drain the spinach and cool, then press out any excess liquid and chop.

Into a bowl put the eggs, egg whites, grated cheese and milk, and whisk together. Stir in the spinach, then season. Spoon the mixture into muffin tins – filling each compartment to no more than three-quarters. Put 3 cubes of feta in each compartment gently pressing down into the mixture.

Bake in the preheated oven for about 15 minutes until the muffins are set and beginning to brown. Serve immediately.

Chick Pea Nibbles with Basil Dip

Serves 4

1 x 400g can of chick peas
6 spring onions, trimmed and chopped
1 beaten egg
½ tsp turmeric
1 tsp ground cumin
1 garlic clove, peeled and crushed
1 tblsp fresh coriander, chopped
salt and pepper
small amount of flour
oil for frying

For the dip:
2 tsp pesto
3 tblsp mayonnaise

Take extra care when deep-fat frying. Hot oil spits wildly and can rise up the sides of the pan very quickly.

Mash the chick peas with a potato masher, then mix with the spring onions in a bowl. Add the egg, turmeric, cumin, garlic and coriander. Mix well together and then season well.

With floured hands shape the mixture into 16 small balls.

Fill a deep saucepan with oil to *no more than one third of its capacity*. Heat the oil, then when hot, fry the nibbles in batches, removing them with a heatproof slotted spoon when golden and draining on kitchen paper. Keep the cooked nibbles in the oven at 150°C (gas mark 2) to warm.

To make the dip – stir the pesto into the mayonnaise, mix well and serve with the warm nibbles.

Greek Tomatoes

Serves 4

4 large beef tomatoes
150g cucumber, peeled and chopped
8 tblsp cooked long grain rice*
salt and pepper
oil to cook
1 garlic clove, peeled and crushed
1 green pepper, de-seeded and finely chopped
75g mushrooms, sliced
2 small onions, peeled and finely chopped

Grease an ovenproof dish. Preheat the oven at 180°C (gas mark 4).

Cut the tops off the tomatoes and set aside. Scoop out the tomato flesh with a small spoon. Chop the pulp of two of the tomatoes and mix with the cucumber and rice. Season well. (The remaining tomato flesh could be used in another dish, or added to a salad.)

Heat some oil and add the garlic and green pepper, then cook for a few minutes and add the mushrooms. Next, add the rice mixture to the pan and cook for 5 minutes. Divide the mixture evenly between the tomato shells and place in an ovenproof dish, putting the tomato lids back on top. Drizzle with olive oil and cook in the preheated oven for 20 minutes, or until the tomatoes are tender.

Meanwhile, fry the onions until they are golden then sprinkle them over the tomatoes to serve.

See page 79 regarding how to store cooked rice correctly.

Stuffed Red Onions

Serves 4

4 large red onions
2 tblsp olive oil
1 garlic clove, peeled and crushed
125g fresh breadcrumbs
50g chopped walnuts
7g fresh thyme leaves
50ml vegetable stock
salt and pepper

To serve:
crusty bread
bag of green salad leaves
balsamic vinegar

Preheat the oven to 200°C (gas mark 6).

Boil the onions in their skins in a large saucepan of water for 15 minutes, then allow to cool. Cut each onion in half through the root and remove the skins. Scoop out the onion flesh with a spoon, leaving two to three layers of onion as a shell. Chop the flesh finely and fry in 1 tblsp oil mixed with the garlic in a frying pan.

Mix together 100g of breadcrumbs, the nuts, thyme leaves and stock, and then add to the onion mix and season. Spoon the mixture into the onion shells and place them in an ovenproof dish with a little water in the bottom. Scatter the remaining breadcrumbs over the top and then drizzle with the remaining olive oil.

Bake in the preheated oven for approximately 15–20 minutes, until beginning to brown. Arrange the salad leaves in a bowl and drizzle lightly with balsamic vinegar.

Serve with crusty bread and the dressed green salad.

Vegetable Tempura

Serves 4

**100g plain flour
salt and pepper
2 eggs
275ml milk and water mixed
sunflower oil for deep frying
100g each of aubergine, broccoli, courgette, mushrooms
and red pepper, cut into bite-size pieces**

To serve:
**250g long grain rice
sweet chilli sauce**

Take extra care when deep-fat frying. Hot oil spits wildly and can rise up the sides of the pan very quickly.

Put the flour in a mixing bowl and season, then make a well in the centre. Gradually add the eggs, beating well. Add the milk mixture little by little, mixing well until the mixture is smooth. Allow to stand in a cool place for 30 minutes.

Preheat the oven to 160°C (gas mark 3).

Fill a deep saucepan with oil to *no more than one third of its capacity.* Then heat it. When the oil is hot, dip the vegetable chunks in the batter mix. Carefully lower the vegetables in small batches into the hot oil and fry for about 5 minutes until golden and crisp. Remove them from the fat with a heatproof slotted spoon and transfer to a baking tray in the preheated oven to keep warm until all the vegetables are cooked.

Meanwhile, cook the rice according to the packet instructions. Serve immediately with the rice and sweet chilli sauce.

Yorkshire Puddings with Red Onion Sauce and Mashed Potatoes

Serves 2

2 medium potatoes, peeled and cut in half
2 red onions, peeled and thinly sliced
1 red pepper, de-seeded and thinly sliced
oil for cooking
6 small frozen Yorkshire puddings
1 vegetable stock cube
1 tsp English mustard
2 tblsp redcurrant jelly
½ glass of red wine
cornflour
knob of butter
1 tblsp milk

Put the potatoes on to boil in a saucepan with a large pinch of salt added to the water, and cook the onions and pepper together in some oil in a frying pan.

Heat the Yorkshire puddings in the oven according to the packet instructions.

Put 250ml boiling water in a measuring jug and crumble in the stock cube, mix well then add the mustard, redcurrant jelly and red wine. Pour into the frying pan with the onions and pepper and keep on a low heat. If the sauce appears too thin, add a little cornflour mixed to a smooth paste with water, to thicken.

When the potatoes are cooked (they usually take about 20 minutes), drain well and mash with the knob of butter and milk. Divide the potatoes between warm plates together with the Yorkshire puddings. Fill the puddings with the onion mixture and serve immediately.

Baby Veg au Gratin

Serves 4

**175g washed baby new potatoes
175g baby carrots
2 leeks, well washed and trimmed
2 sticks of celery
100g mange-tout
300ml milk
25g butter
2 tblsp plain flour
2 tsp wholegrain mustard
125g full-fat soft cheese with garlic and herbs
salt and pepper
fresh breadcrumbs
75g Cheddar cheese, grated**

Cut the potatoes into 1cm slices and slice the carrots, leeks and celery diagonally to a similar size.

In a saucepan, bring the potatoes and carrots to the boil and simmer for 5 minutes, then add the leeks and celery. Simmer for a further 5 minutes until the vegetables are just tender, then add the mange-tout.

Heat the milk and butter in a saucepan, stirring to prevent burning. Whisk in the flour to make the sauce smooth, and continue whisking until the sauce thickens. Remove from the heat and add the mustard and soft cheese. Season to taste.

Drain the vegetables well and put in a large shallow ovenproof dish, then pour the sauce over the vegetables. Mix together the breadcrumbs and grated cheese and add to the dish. Grill until the cheese and breadcrumbs turn golden.

Sweet and Savoury Kebabs

Serves 4

12 wooden kebab sticks
1 courgette
1 apple
1 yellow or orange pepper, de-seeded
1 red onion, peeled
1 small pack of feta cheese
12 cherry tomatoes
12 button mushrooms
24 mange-tout or sugar-snap peas
olive oil

To serve:
sweet chilli dip

Soak the kebab sticks in water for at least 30 minutes – this will prevent the wood from burning as the kebabs are cooked.

Cut the courgette, apple, pepper, red onion and feta cheese into slices or chunks, roughly the same size as the cherry tomatoes and mushrooms. Layer the apple, vegetables and cheese onto the kebab sticks, placing one mange-tout or sugar-snap pea either side of the feta cheese.

Kebabs can be cooked under a hot grill or on a barbecue. To grill: place the kebabs in a grill pan and drizzle with plenty of olive oil. Spoon some olive oil over the kebabs from time to time whilst cooking – paying particular attention to the cheese and mushrooms. If cooking on a barbecue, turn frequently and drizzle with olive oil. The kebabs are ready when the cheese is beginning to turn brown and the vegetables are softened.

Serve with a sweet chilli dip.

Cheese and Onion Balls

Makes about 20

**25g butter
water
50g flour
2 eggs
50g cheese, grated
1 small onion, peeled and finely chopped
salt and pepper
oil for deep frying**

To serve:
selection of fresh dips

Take extra care when deep-fat frying. Hot oil spits wildly and can rise up the sides of the pan very quickly.

Heat the butter in a saucepan and add 4 tblsp of boiling water. Remove from the heat and stir in the flour until the mixture forms a soft ball and leaves the sides of the pan clean. Leave to cool.

Gradually beat the eggs into the mixture until it is shiny and will stand in soft peaks. Add the cheese and onion and season, mixing well.

Take a large saucepan, and fill to one third with oil and heat. To test if the fat is hot enough, drop a small cube of bread into the oil: when it starts to bubble, the oil is hot enough for deep frying. Carefully drop teaspoonfuls of the mixture into the hot oil and fry in batches of five for about 5 minutes until golden brown. Remove from the oil with a heatproof slotted spoon and drain on kitchen paper. Serve immediately with dips.

You can also make this dish up in advance, and refrigerate. When required, spread the cheese and onion balls on a baking tray, warm through in the oven at 180°C (gas mark 4) for about 10–12 minutes, then serve.

INDEX

A
Artichoke Bake, 85
Aubergine and Mozzarella Grills, 87
  Slices, Golden, 92
Aubergines, Cheesy Leeks and, 91
  with Tomato Sauce, Stuffed, 97
Avocado with Brie, Hot, 32

B
Baby Veg au Gratin, 121
Bake, Artichoke, 85
  , Broccoli, 75
  , Crispy Mushroom, 80
  , Tomato and Potato, 44
  , Vegetable Rice, 78
  with Green Vegetables, Coconut Potato, 43
Baked Beetroot, 84
  Potato Slices, 38
  Potatoes, Stuffed, 46
  Sweet Potatoes with Green Salad, 50
Banana Grills, 14
Bean Bake, Curried, 94
Beans, Mexican Re-Fried, 86
Beetroot, Baked, 84
Broccoli Bake, 75
Bruschetta, Tomato and Mushroom, 20
  with Olives and Cherry Tomatoes, 22
Bubble and Squeak, 42
Burgers, Meat-Free, 113

C
Casserole, Crunchy Topped Vegetable, 81
Celery and Onion Ramekins, 29
Chargrilled Vegetables with Rice, 110
Cheese and Apple Snacks, 16
  and Onion Balls, 123
  and Onion Jackets with Tomato Salad, 52
  , Celery and Onion Pancakes, 34
  Pudding, 74
Cheesy Leeks and Aubergines, 91
  Zucchini, 111
Chick Pea Nibbles with Basil Dip, 116
Chilli Mix with Potato and Carrot Mash, 95
  Noodles, 109
  , Vegetarian, 82
Coconut Potato Bake with Green Vegetables, 43
Coleslaw, Pink, 36
Courgette and Cream Cheese Pâté, 32
Courgettes and Corn in Lemon Sauce with Spicy Couscous, 90
Creamy Cheese Pizza, 102
Crispy Mushroom Bake, 80
Crumble, Tomato, 88
Crunchy Topped Vegetable Casserole, 81
Curried Bean Bake, 94
  Jackets, 48

D
Deep-Fried Brie with Kiwi, 100

E
Egg and Potato Mornay, 49
Eggy Bread, 21

F
Feta and Potato Cakes, 47
Focaccia Pizza, 103
Frittata, Red and Green, 101
Fritters, Sweetcorn, 77

G
Golden Aubergine Slices, 92
Greek Tomatoes, 117
Grilled Ricotta with Sun-Dried Tomatoes, 26

H
Halloumi with Tomatoes, Hot, 24
Home-Made Onion Rings with Pink Coleslaw, 36
Hot Avocado with Brie, 32
  Halloumi with Tomatoes, 24
  Pasta Salad, 63

J
Jackets, Curried, 48
  with Tomato Salad, Cheese and Onion, 52

K
Kebabs, Sweet and Savoury, 122

L
Leeky Potatoes, 39
Lemony Tomatoes with Rice and Bean Salad, 112
Linguine with Lemon Sauce, 56

M
Meat-Free Burgers, 113
Mediterranean Spaghetti, 61
Mexican Re-Fried Beans, 86
Mornay, Egg and Potato, 49
Mushroom and Pine Nut Pasta, 65
  Bake, Crispy, 80
  Brunch, 27
  Grill, 23
  Hollows, 30
  Pâté, 33
  Stroganoff, 76
Mushrooms in Garlic Butter, 15
  with Lemon Couscous, Pesto, 108
Mozzarella and Cranberry Toasts, 17
  Melts, 12

Muffins, Spinach and Feta, 115

N
Noodles, Chilli, 109
  , Sweet and Sour, 83
Nutty Stilton Tart, 107
  Tortellini, 64

O
Omelette, Potato and Pea, 41
Onion Rings with Pink Coleslaw, Home-made, 36
  Soup with Cheese Rafts, Red, 31
Onions, Stuffed Red, 118

P
Paella, 89
Pancakes, Cheese, Celery and Onion, 34
  , Tomato and Mushroom, 35
Panini Parcels, 28
Parsnip and Potato Pieces with Red Salad, 53
Pasta Gratin with Red Cheese, 69
  , Mushroom and Pine Nut, 65
  Pronto!, 62
  , Red Pepper, 67
  Salad, Hot, 63
  Stuffed Peppers, 73
  with Aubergine and Ricotta, 68
  with Melted Brie, Penne, 66
Pâté, Courgette and Cream Cheese, 32
  , Mushroom, 33
  , Tuna, 33
Penne Pasta with Melted Brie, 66
Pepper Pesto Toasties, 19
Peppers, Pasta Stuffed, 73
  , Savoury Rice Filled, 72
Pesto Mushrooms with Lemon Couscous, 108
Pineapple Toasties, 18
Pizza, Creamy Cheese, 102
  , Focaccia, 103
  , Roast Vegetable, 104
Potato and Pea Omelette, 41
  Bake, Tomato and, 44
  Bake with Green Vegetables, Coconut, 43
  Cakes, Feta and, 47
  Mornay, Egg and, 49
  Skins with Soured Cream Dip, 40
  Slices, Baked, 38

Potatoes, Leeky, 39
, Stuffed Baked, 46

R

Radishes with Garlic Bread, Stir Fry, 93
Red and Green Frittata, 101
    Onion and Pepper Tarts, 105
    Onion Soup with Cheese Rafts, 31
    Pepper Pasta, 67
Ratatouille with Spicy Couscous, 96
Rice and Bean Salad, Lemony Tomatoes with, 112
, Savoury Tuna, 79
Supper, Savoury, 99
Roast Vegetable Pizza, 104
Rösti with Poached Egg and Green Beans, 51

S

Salsa Nachos, 35
Savoury Rice Filled Peppers, 72
    Rice Supper, 99
    Tuna Rice, 79
Spaghetti, Mediterranean, 61
Spinach and Feta Muffins, 115
Stilton Tart, Nutty
Stir Fry Radishes with Garlic Bread, 93
Stroganoff, Mushroom, 76
Stuffed Aubergines with Tomato Sauce, 97
    Baked Potatoes, 46
    Red Onions, 118
Sweet and Savoury Kebabs, 122
    and Sour Noodles, 83
    Potatoes with Green Salad, Baked, 50
Sweetcorn Fritters, 77

T

Tagliatelle and Cider Mushrooms, 58
, Tuna, 57
with Blue Cheese Sauce and Crispy Onions, 60
with Herby Green Sauce, 59

Tart, Nutty Stilton, 107
, Tomato Stilton and Mozzarella, 106
Tarts, Red Onion and Pepper, 105
Toasties, Pepper Pesto, 19
, Pineapple, 18
Tomato and Mushroom Bruschetta, 20
    and Mushroom Pancakes, 35
    and Potato Bake, 44
    Brunch, 13
    Crumble, 88
    Salsa and Tzatziki with Tortilla Chips, 25
, Stilton and Mozzarella Tart, 106
Tomatoes, Greek, 117
    with Cheese Soufflé Filling, 98
    with Rice and Bean Salad, Lemony, 112
Tortellini, Nutty, 64
Tuna Pâté, 33
    Rice, Savoury, 79
    Tagliatelle, 57

V

Veg au Gratin, Baby, 121
Vegetable Casserole, Crunchy Topped, 81
    Pizza, Roast, 104
    Rice Bake, 78
    Tempura, 119
Vegetables, Wild Rice with Roast, 114
    with Rice, Chargrilled, 110
Vegetarian Chilli, 82

W

Wedges N Eggs, 45
Wild Rice with Roast Vegetables, 114

Y

Yorkshire Puddings with Red Onion Sauce and Mashed Potatoes, 120

Z

Zucchini, Cheesy, 111

In the same series

HOW TO BOIL AN EGG
and 184 other simple recipes for one

If you don't consider yourself a cook, this book is for you! It tells you all you need to know to cook for yourself – not just how to boil an egg, but how to poach, scramble or fry it as well! It also tells you how to prepare and cook vegetables and about different meats, and includes recipes and suggestions for a great variety of snacks and main meals.

Originally written for Jan Arkless's son when he first went to university, her recipes are quick, easy and economical to make. Most are geared towards feeding one person but there are a few recipes which cater for two people, so you can entertain as well as feed yourself.

NO MEAT FOR ME, PLEASE!
Recipes for the Vegetarian in the Family

This book is purpose-written for the family which includes a vegetarian among its members. It enables the cook to provide single vegetarian dishes alongside the meat course which the rest of the family is eating, with no fuss or inconvenience. Those new to catering for the vegetarian in the family will love the ease with which they can incorporate these dishes into their usual routine.

As most of the recipes feed single portions, the book is also a great stand-alone vegetarian cookbook for those vegetarians living on their own. They will love the mouthwatering range of starters, snacks, roasts, main courses, sauces and dips included here.

Uniform with this book